Walking the Jerusalem Circuit

Walking the Jerusalem Circuit

In the Footsteps of Pilgrims Before the Crusades

RODNEY AIST

CASCADE Books • Eugene, Oregon

WALKING THE JERUSALEM CIRCUIT
In the Footsteps of Pilgrims Before the Crusades

Copyright © 2025 Rodney Aist. All rights reserved. Except for brief quotations in critical publications or reviews, no part of this book may be reproduced in any manner without prior written permission from the publisher. Write: Permissions, Wipf and Stock Publishers, 199 W. 8th Ave., Suite 3, Eugene, OR 97401.

Cascade Books
An Imprint of Wipf and Stock Publishers
199 W. 8th Ave., Suite 3
Eugene, OR 97401

www.wipfandstock.com

PAPERBACK ISBN: 978-1-6667-7101-5
HARDCOVER ISBN: 978-1-6667-7102-2
EBOOK ISBN: 978-1-6667-7103-9

Cataloguing-in-Publication data:

Names: Aist, Rodney, author.

Title: Walking the Jerusalem Circuit : in the footsteps of pilgrims before the Crusades / Rodney Aist.

Description: Eugene, OR: Cascade Books, 2025 | Includes bibliographical references and index.

Identifiers: ISBN 978-1-6667-7101-5 (paperback) | ISBN 978-1-6667-7102-2 (hardcover) | ISBN 978-1-6667-7103-9 (ebook)

Subjects: LCSH: Christian pilgrims and pilgrimages. | Sacred space. | Israel—Description and travel.

Classification: BX2320.5I75 A58 2025 (paperback) | BX2320 (ebook)

07/01/25

For their scholarship and encouragement:

Thomas O'Loughlin
John Wilkinson (in memoriam)

Richard and JulieAnn Sewell
Janet Manio

Contents

Preface | ix

Abbreviations | xv

1. The Jerusalem Circuit | 1
2. Practicalities and Logistics | 24
3. The Stations | 35
   Entering Jerusalem | 37
   Stations 1–5: The Holy Sepulchre | 41
   Station 1: The Tomb of Christ | 49
   Station 2: Golgotha | 57
   Station 3: The Holy Cross | 69
   Station 4: The Center of the World | 75
   Station 5: Mary the Egyptian | 80
   Stations 6–7: The Church of Holy Sion | 84
   Station 6: The Cenacle | 90
   Station 7: The Dormition Abbey | 97
   Station 8: The Church of Holy Wisdom: Jesus' Trial Before Pilate | 104
   Stations 9–10: The Church of St. Anne | 111
   Station 9: The Pool of Bethesda | 113
   Station 10: The Nativity of Mary | 119
   Station 11: The Jephonias Monument | 123
   Station 12: The Church of Mary's Tomb | 128
   Station 13: The Grotto of Gethsemane | 133
   Station 14: The Church of Gethsemane | 139
   Station 15: The Eleona | 147

Contents

    Station 16: The Church of the Ascension | 154
    Concluding the Circuit | 162

4. Bibliography | 165

Preface

The purpose of *Walking the Jerusalem Circuit* is to revive a former Christian practice: the pre-Crusader pilgrim circuit of Jerusalem (the Jerusalem Circuit).[1] Approximately four kilometers (2.5 miles) long, the Circuit connected the principal Christian sites in a logical walking order that could be done in less than a day. In doing so, it didn't always follow the narrative movements of Jesus, though it ultimately progressed from his death and resurrection to his heavenly ascension. The Circuit also included extrabiblical traditions that were and remain important to Christians around the world but may be less familiar to some.

Walking the Jerusalem Circuit today is ideal for those already familiar with the holy sites as it provides a different type of experience than first-time pilgrims and short-term visitors are generally seeking. There are better ways to initially encounter the holy places, such as seeing the sites at a slower pace, visiting certain places in a different order, and not walking *up* the Mount of Olives! What the Jerusalem Circuit offers is a fresh (if ancient) way of engaging familiar sites and well-known biblical events, providing a unique framework for reflecting upon Christian Jerusalem, past and present.

Since the biblical and historical material associated with the sites is considerably broad, curiosity may inspire further inquiry, making it a study pilgrimage of sorts. More holistically, walking the Circuit is an embodied exercise that embraces the physicality of pilgrimage, the nexus of biblical place and story, the sights and sounds of the city, and the thoughts and prayers that emerge. Just as pilgrims of the past encountered God through a range of practices, walking the Circuit today integrates the contemporary appeal for physical walking and embodied forms of spirituality with intellectual

---

1. Use of the term Jerusalem Circuit follows John Wilkinson. The adjective forms of pilgrim and pilgrimage will be used interchangeably, e.g., pilgrim/age circuit and pilgrim/age texts.

curiosity, devotional reflection, and prayers for the contemporary city. In doing so, the Jerusalem Circuit becomes a micro-pilgrimage of macro dimensions. As you walk the Jerusalem Circuit may God "keep your going out and your coming in from this time on and forevermore" (Ps 121:8).

JERUSALEM BEFORE THE CRUSADES

Walking the Jerusalem Circuit focuses on Christian Jerusalem before the Crusades, which we'll divide into two periods, the Byzantine (325–638) and the Early Islamic (638–1099). The Byzantine period denotes the transition of the Roman Empire into one of Christian rule with its capital based in Constantinople accompanied by a shift from Latin to Greek as its dominant language. Although Greek Constantinople did not fall until 1453, for Jerusalem, the Byzantine period, which oversaw the development of the Christian Holy Land, lasted for three centuries ending with the Arab conquest of 636–38. The Christianization of the Holy Land included the extensive building of churches and shrines, the establishment of Palestinian monasticism, the development of the stational liturgy of Jerusalem, and the popularization of Christian pilgrimage.[2]

Historical periods are subjective. One could end the Byzantine period in 614, the year the Sassanid Persians conquered Jerusalem, capturing the relic of the Holy Cross. Although Christian reports of the conquest, which include numerical lists of victims and references to specific churches, describe scenes of destruction and massacre, the archeological evidence for the damage or destruction of churches is limited.[3] After Byzantine authority was restored in 628, most of the Christian sites were repaired by the patriarch Modestus (d. c. 631), and with a couple of exceptions, the Christian commemorative landscape survived Persian occupation. The restoration was short lived, with Byzantine rule coming to an end by 638. Unlike the Persian siege, the Arab conquest was a peaceful affair with the Christian patriarch Sophronius (d. c. 638) handing the keys of the city over to the Muslim caliph 'Umar (d. 644).[4]

The years between the Persian and Arab conquests are also known as the Interconquest period (614–38). Along with the rebuilding program of Modestus, the period is notable for the restoration of the Holy Cross on

---

2. See Wilken, *Land Called Holy*.
3. Schick, *Christian Communities*, 33–39.
4. Scholars differ on the dates of the Arab conquest by a year or two.

PREFACE

March 21, most likely in 630, by the emperor Heraclius (d. 641), and at least two monuments related to the Circuit were likely built at the time (see stations 3, 4, and 11).

Although certain places were diminished following the conquests—and at least one church on the Circuit was abandoned—Christian pilgrimage continued throughout the Early Islamic period with pilgrim descriptions of major sites, like the Holy Sepulchre and the Church of the Ascension, essentially on par with Byzantine accounts, particularly with regard to commemorative detail and religious imagination.[5] The *Commemoratorium* (c. 808), a report on the Christian presence in Jerusalem and the Holy Land during the reign of Charlemagne (d. 814), shows that Christian institutions were flourishing at the time. However, earthquakes remained a problem (e.g., in 633, 749, 1033), and while Early Islamic rulers were generally tolerant of other religions, Muslim–Christian relations became more strained as time went on, culminating in the destruction of the Holy Sepulchre in 1009 on the orders of the Fatimid caliph Hakim (d. 1021).

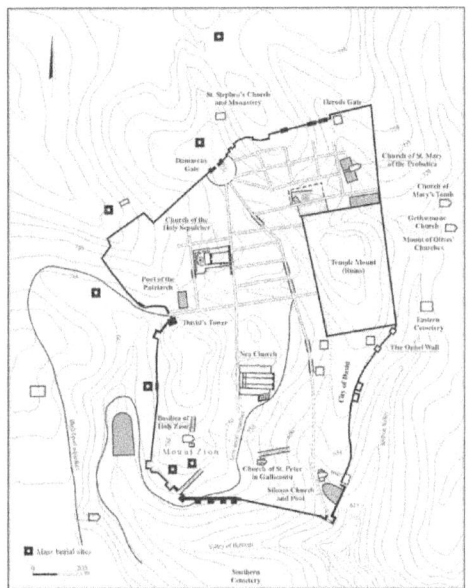

Fig. 1. Plan of Jerusalem in the Byzantine period. From E. Stern (ed.), *The New Encyclopedia of Archaeological Excavations in the Holy Land*, 2:769. With permission of the Israel Exploration Society.

5. References to the Holy Sepulchre denote the complex as a whole and are never used to specifically refer to the tomb of Christ.

Preface

THE LANGUAGE OF COMMEMORATION

Pre-Crusader sources commonly use the language of veneration or adoration. Veneration (to honor, to respect, to revere) doesn't necessarily imply the same as worship, though the word will be strange or uncomfortable for some. Instead, the book employs the language of commemoration, which most simply refers to an act of remembrance.

Whether at home or in the Holy Land, Christianity is a religion of memory: remembering the mighty deeds and mercy of God and the life and ministry of Christ. Indeed, it's a religion of *repetitive* memory, which occurs through ritual and liturgy and the cyclical nature of the Christian calendar: rereading Scripture and retelling the stories of faith. While we remember through individual acts, commemoration often implies a form of shared or collective memory; it's something we commonly do with others from simple words to embodied actions and physical expressions of memory. It may be tied to a particular setting or enacted apart from where the memory originally took shape. Commemoration recognizes the *importance* of a subject—e.g., a place, event, story, or person—but it lacks the connotation of veneration or worship.

Just as place is often a concomitant feature of commemoration, Holy Land pilgrimage embraces the idea of commemorating biblical events "at the very spot" (or traditional location) where they occurred. For pilgrims, places mattered, as they still do today. Notwithstanding the association of miracles with certain places or the granting of indulgences for particular destinations, Christianity has never espoused a theology that denies the omnipresence of God nor advocated the existence of intrinsically holy places that are qualitatively more sacred than other spaces. That is not to say that notions of space and place aren't important; the basic tenet of incarnational theology embraces the particularly of place, while theophanies and consecrated ("set aside") places are part of Christian experience and practice.

Some traditions are comfortable with the language of veneration and the recognition of "sacred" places; for others, both are questionable. Even if it's merely "remembering" what others believe(d), hopefully, a commemorative approach will allow otherwise hesitant participants to more fully enter the religious imagination of the Jerusalem Circuit, including places and stories associated with Jesus, Mary, and the early church.[6] Theology, in

---

6. All references to Mary indicate the mother of Jesus unless otherwise noted.

Preface

the end, is about finding language, frames, and lenses that help us engage lived experience in more curious and meaningful ways. For the Jerusalem Circuit, this concerns both the religious worldview of the past and the intermingling of heaven and earth in front of our eyes.

COMMEMORATING THE STATIONS

The book begins by presenting the evidence for the Jerusalem Circuit (section 1), followed by a short section on the practicalities of the walk (section 2), before preceding to the heart of the book: the stations of the Jerusalem Circuit (section 3). Each "station chapter" contains background information on the site, suggestions for commemorating the station, pilgrimage texts, relevant Scriptures, and thoughts for reflection. Along with history, archaeology, and architecture, attention is given to commemorative details, including contemporary art, sculptures, and images.

To commemorate a station, find an appropriate location at or near the site to read the corresponding material. Individuals can do this inside churches; group readings and prayers should be done outside (a couple of exceptions are permitted). Then, proceed with the station.

The book resources an immersive experience that appeals to Scripture, history, pilgrim traditions, contemporary images, and personal reflection. Although *Walking the Jerusalem Circuit* covers a lot of ground, the intent is not to prescribe the experience nor overwhelm it with words. Commemorate each station however you choose: from skipping or tweaking the material to focusing on silent prayer. Be creative, or simply enjoy the walk. While the book facilitates a physical exercise, there are virtual ways to engage the sites and narratives of the Circuit from further readings to related videos. Finally, many will note that the language of stations is also used for the Via Dolorosa, i.e., the Stations of the Cross. Although they are both stational walks, the history, content, and purpose of the Jerusalem Circuit are significantly different from the Via Dolorosa.

IMAGES OF JERUSALEM

Walking the Circuit is a venture in exploring images of Jerusalem, past and present, layered and broken, sacred and divine: from the time of Jesus, to the pre-Crusader period, to the modern-day city. For Christian pilgrims, there is a tension between the real and the imagined city, between our

PREFACE

childhood impressions and the rocks on the ground. While the sites can elicit both clarity and dissonance (often at the same time!), Holy Land pilgrimage is not about resolving the tensions of how we perceive the city but about increasing our capacity for holding multivalent images together, while the theological task, especially for church leaders, is to translate the particularities of Holy Land stories to people and places back home.

The figures in the book add to the mix. A few of the images are co-terminous with the pre-Crusader circuit. These include the Madaba Map (c. 600) and the eighth-century mosaic of Jerusalem from the Church of St. Stephen at Umm ar-Rasas, Jordan (figs. 2 and 5). Three plans of Jerusalem churches are from Adomnán's *On the Holy Places*—the Holy Sepulchre, Holy Sion, and the Church of the Ascension.[7] While the prototypes date to the late seventh century (not extant), the images (figs. 6, 14, and 23) are from a ninth-century manuscript in the Österreichische Nationalbibliothek in Vienna. The illustration of Jerusalem from the Bayerischen Staatsbibliothek in Munich (mid-twelfth century) accompanies Bede's *On the Holy Places* (early eighth century), which in turn is derived from the Adomnán text (late seventh century).[8]

The pilgrim ampulla (sixth or seventh century) from the diocesan museum in Monza, Italy (fig. 9), is of personal interest; its depiction of the aedicule (the tomb of Christ) is the logo for St. George's College, Jerusalem, where I serve as course director. Also related are modern drawings of the Byzantine complex of the Holy Sepulchre and of the Gethsemane churches through the ages (figs. 7 and 21), while the twentieth-century mosaic of Willibald in the Dormition Abbey portrays one of the Circuit's central protagonists (fig. 15). The illustrations also include Crusader maps and art from the late Middle Ages and the early modern period. While they do not belong to the pre-Crusader material, they hopefully contribute to general reflections on the image of Jerusalem, past and present.

---

7. Following the pilgrim texts, Sion will be spelled with an *s* throughout the book.

8. There has been significant confusion about the image (fig. 11), which has been inerrantly identified as a late seventh-century depiction of Jerusalem. Although the twelfth-century image is ultimately based on Adomnán's description of a column associated with both the legend of the Holy Cross and the center of the world, it is an original twelfth-century drawing and does not represent an earlier prototype. Compare Bede, *On the Holy Places* 2, with Adomnán, *On the Holy Places* 1.11.

Abbreviations

Gen	Genesis
Deut	Deuteronomy
2 Sam	2 Samuel
1 Kgs	1 Kings
2 Chr	2 Chronicles
Neh	Nehemiah
Ps	Psalms
Prov	Proverbs
Song	Song of Songs
Isa	Isaiah
Dan	Daniel
Zech	Zechariah
Matt	Matthew
1 Cor	1 Corinthians
Rev	Revelation

I.

The Jerusalem Circuit

FOLLOW THE ROUTE THAT Christian pilgrims took through the Holy City centuries ago; visit the primary sites of Christian Jerusalem in the same sequence as pilgrims before the Crusades. The pre-Crusader pilgrim circuit of Jerusalem (the Jerusalem Circuit) brings together early medieval Jerusalem and the New Testament past. Commemorating events in the life of Christ and the early church, the route allows one to walk in the footsteps of those who walked in the footsteps of Jesus.

That said, doing the Circuit today is a modern exercise that appeals to a historical practice rather than a re-creation of a medieval experience. Traditionally, pilgrims did not come to simply "revivify" the Bible but were interested in the Jerusalem of their time, and the same should be true today. Perceiving the holy sites as testimonies to God's actions in the past, they were also attuned to the city's contemporary witness to God's eternal providence as well as the eschatological resonance, or future hope, conveyed by the city and its sites. Pilgrims sought New Jerusalem in stone, and Christian Jerusalem obliged: it was a walled city without a temple containing the throne (tomb) of Christ (Rev 21–22). While pilgrims imagined the city as a projection of New Jerusalem, what they actually experienced was an intermingled city, a city both past and present, of heaven and earth, awaiting its final redemption. Walking the Jerusalem Circuit invites us to prayerfully observe the city today: its people and places, its problems, hopes, and aspirations.

To qualify the point: unlike those who come to the Holy Land looking for an unmediated experience with the New Testament Jesus, pre-Crusader pilgrims were equally focused on the present, seeking God in the contemporary conditions of their day. In this sense, pilgrim tradition can help us more fully encounter what we see around us. On the other hand, pilgrim writers viewed the world in their own terms: "Jewish sources mention Jews, Christians mention Christians, and Muslims mention Muslim, but 'the other' is treated as if he did not exist."[1] Pilgrim tradition can guide us in important ways, but we can also do better: recognizing the Abrahamic faiths in various ways on the walk.

Despite the theological polemics that plagued both Eastern and Western Christianity, the pre-Crusader pilgrim accounts place little attention on divisions within the church. They seldom comment on differences. Stated more positively, Latin pilgrims engaged Eastern traditions and participated in Holy Land liturgies as if they were their own, presenting the church as a unified whole. In the same way, the spirit of *Walking the Jerusalem Circuit* is the ecumenical unity of the Christian church.

A significant part of *Walking the Jerusalem Circuit* are the pilgrimage texts, which convey the thoughts and practices of past pilgrims, including their physical engagement of the sites, their religious imagination, and the role of material objects as spiritual blessings. Egeria (380s) shares her enthusiasm about traveling through the Holy Land escorted by monks who served as pilgrim guides: "What I admire and value most is that all the hymns and antiphons and readings . . . are always relevant . . . to the place in which they are used. They never fail to be appropriate." Egeria expresses what Holy Land pilgrims now take for granted: the tradition of reading Scripture on site. At Cana in Galilee where Jesus turned water into wine, the sixth-century Piacenza Pilgrim reenacted part of the miracle: "Two of the water jugs are there. I filled one of them with wine, lifted it onto my shoulders and offered it at the altar. We washed in the very spring for a blessing." Inside the tomb of Christ, he filled a souvenir ampulla with oil: "A bronze lamp burns day and night at the place where his head was; we took a blessing from the lamp and put it back in its place." Elsewhere he measured stone impressions of Jesus' palms, fingers, and footprints with strings, while Arculf (680s) calculated the size of Jesus' tomb with his hands.[2]

---

1. Murphy-O'Connor, *Keys to Jerusalem*, 225, which cites my work on Willibald: Aist, *Christian Topography*, 245. Despite the physical prominence of the Dome of the Rock, Willibald never mentions the Islamic presence in the city, portraying Jerusalem exclusively in Christian terms.

2. Egeria, *Travels* 47.5; Piacenza Pilgrim, *Travels* 4, 18, 22, and 23; Adomnán, *On the Holy Places* 1.2.

More generally, Byzantine Christians embraced the idea of being bodily present in the holy places. Cyril of Jerusalem (d. 386) told his catechumens: "Others merely hear, we see and touch," while Paulinus of Nola (d. 431) writes with excitement: "No other sentiment draws people to Jerusalem than the desire to see and touch the places where Christ was physically present, and to be able to say from their very own experience, 'We have gone into his tabernacle, and have worshipped in the places where his feet have stood.'"[3] Pilgrim writings, together with Scripture, will guide us along the way.

THE JERUSALEM CIRCUIT BEFORE THE CRUSADES

The Circuit

The evidence for a pre-Crusader walking route is represented by a group of independent texts that describe the sites in the same sequence. Four texts are of particular importance: Sophronius (before 614), *The Armenian Guide* (c. 630), Willibald (724–26), and Bernard the Monk (870), discussed below. While we know that individual pilgrims, like Willibald, walked the route in question, the evidence suggests that the Circuit was a recognized practice of Jerusalem pilgrimage over several hundred years. The aforementioned texts cover a three-century span from the late Byzantine to the Early Islamic period, a time consisting of both Christian and Muslim rule. They include Latin, Greek, and Armenian writings, indicating broad participation among the pilgrim communities of Jerusalem. The types of texts are also diverse, consisting of a poem composed by a resident of Jerusalem (Sophronius), accounts written or dictated by pilgrims (Willibald and Bernard), and an impersonal pilgrim guide (*The Armenian Guide*).

To be clear, the sources never mention the phenomenon of a standardized circuit. What we have are multiple independent sources describing the same route in walking terms. *The Armenian Guide* refers to steps and paces, while Sophronius, Willibald, and Bernard are depicted walking the sites they describe. Indeed, the three-century time span, the diversity of languages, and the differing genres of the texts allow us to speculate further on the practice, beginning with the assumption that the Circuit was supported by the Jerusalem church. While pilgrims would have also walked it

---

3. Cyril of Jerusalem, *Catechesis* 13.22; Paulinus of Nola, *Letter* 49.14.

on their own, we can think in terms of language-specific or multilingual tours organized by Jerusalem's resident monks that presumably occurred on a near-daily basis or at least multiple times per week.

The function of the Circuit was straightforward: to link the primary sites of the Holy City in a convenient order in "one go." The Circuit that eventually emerged began at the Holy Sepulchre, preceded to Holy Sion, continued to Gethsemane, and ended on the summit of the Mount of Olives. Such a route—namely, the movement from Holy Sion to Gethsemane—forced a basic decision: which way to take around the former Temple Mount, an area of some thirty-six acres (fourteen hectares; 140 dunams) on the eastern side of the city. Although Byzantine Christians did not develop or visit the site—they viewed the ruins as the fulfillment of Jesus' prophecy concerning the temple's destruction—its size and location required pilgrims to make a choice regarding the route from Mount Sion to Gethsemane.

They could either go around the southeast corner of the Temple Mount: heading east down or parallel to the Hinnom Valley before walking north up the Jehoshaphat Valley,[4] passing Aceldama, the pool of Siloam, and some monumental tombs along the way.[5] Or, they could go through the heart of the city, skirting the northwest corner of the Temple Mount—stopping at the Church of Holy Wisdom (Jesus' trial before Pilate), the pool of Bethesda, and Mary's birthplace—before exiting through the eastern gate. As the Circuit developed, it chose the latter option, which had easier pathways and more significant sites.

Progressing from the Holy Sepulchre to the Mount of Olives, it was not possible to include every site on a single itinerary. As a result, places not on the Circuit, such as Aceldama and the pool of Siloam, eventually assumed a second-tier status. However, pilgrims, who sojourned in the city for weeks at a time, would eventually visit these sites. Once the Circuit was established, new commemorations appeared on the route (see station 11).

The Circuit consisted of places and stories of Jesus, Mary, and the early church. While the route began with the Holy Sepulchre and ended on the

---

4. The Kidron Valley runs from Jerusalem to the Dead Sea. The section of the Kidron between Gethsemane and the pool of Siloam has also been traditionally known as the Jehoshaphat Valley (see Joel 3:2), which is its common designation in the pilgrim texts.

5. The tombs of the Jehoshaphat Valley include funerary monuments known today as the tombs of Absalom, Zechariah, and Benei Hezir. They have been associated in Christian tradition with the tombs of Simeon, James the brother of Jesus, and various Old Testament figures.

top of the Mount of Olives, the sequence of stations was determined by the location and proximity of the sites. As a result, certain narratives were out of order. But that was never the point: other than the ultimate progression from resurrection to ascension, the route was established by basic topographical considerations—the locations of the principal sites conveniently mapped upon the city's network of intramural streets and extramural pathways creating a standardized route that pilgrims could complete in a day.

The Circuit was separate from the stational liturgy of the Jerusalem Church, which used various churches, or stations, as places of worship: the lectionary not only listed readings for the day but also assigned the station (location) of the service.[6] Moving from church to church, Jerusalem worship in the Byzantine period was public and processional. Pilgrims, in turn, timed their movements to be present at the "actual place" for the major feasts (e.g., in Jerusalem for Easter, Ascension, Pentecost, and the feast of the Holy Cross; in Bethlehem for Christmas; at the Jordan River for Epiphany).

The Jerusalem Circuit was a different practice, albeit one with a strong devotional focus. Although it's possible that prayers and readings were developed for the Circuit, pilgrims prayed on their own. Sophronius's poems describe his veneration and prostration at the sites. The Willibald text explicitly mentions that he prayed at Holy Sion and the tomb of Mary, and he presumably did so at every site.

Texts not structured according to the route inform, nonetheless, our understanding of the Circuit and pilgrim visitation at the sites. Adomnán of Iona (d. 704) incorporated the oral account of the seventh-century pilgrim Arculf into his treatise *De locis sanctis* (*On the Holy Places*). During his nine-month sojourn in Jerusalem (680s), Arculf was "tireless in making pilgrimage to the holy places." He frequented the Holy Sepulchre and the Church of Mary's Tomb and was a "constant pilgrim" at the Church of the Ascension. Not only did pilgrims pray at the sites, they visited places over and over. Just as Christianity is a religion of repetitive memory, visiting the sites—and walking the Circuit—was something that pilgrims repeated.[7]

This brings us to an intriguing dynamic of the Willibald text. Willibald dictated his account of Jerusalem to the nun Hugeburc, at the age of

---

6. See *Armenian Lectionary*.

7. See Adomnán, *On the Holy Places* 1.2, 1.12, and 1.23. The Adomnán text incorporates the contemporary report of the pilgrim Arculf with earlier written sources from the library of Iona.

seventy-eight *over fifty years after* his pilgrimage to the Holy Land. *Every* site that Willibald mentions is on the route; similarly, no sites are included that are off the route. It appears that the Jerusalem Circuit—which Willibald presumably walked multiple times—was so firmly etched in his mind that he could use it as a mnemonic device a half-century after his visit! Even if Willibald used some previously written notes (there is no evidence that he did), the text's account of Jerusalem, which Hugeburc subsequently composed, exclusively follows the route.

As noted with Adomnán, not every pilgrimage text follows the template of the Jerusalem Circuit. Numerous factors influenced the composition of a text, and there were many ways to order the sites of the city. For instance, whereas the Circuit proceeds from the Holy Sepulchre *outward*, some texts move *toward* the Holy Sepulchre. That said, the existence of differently structured texts does not undermine the argument.

To summarize the case for the Jerusalem Circuit, a selection of independent texts consisting of multiple languages spanning more than three centuries traces a common route through the city in their ordering of the holy sites, suggesting that a standardized pilgrim circuit existed in pre-Crusader Jerusalem. Not only does the ordering of the material follow a logical walking route that corresponds to major streets of the city (see below), the texts employ the language of personal movement. The evidence points to a recognized practice that was formative to the pre-Crusader experience of Jerusalem; at the very least, one can knowingly walk in the footsteps of actual pilgrims, namely, Sophronius, Willibald, and Bernard the Monk.

The Madaba Map

Before turning to the stations—and then to the principal texts—we'll introduce the Madaba Map (c. 600), a remarkable visual source for walking the Jerusalem Circuit today. The map is a mosaic of the Holy Land on the floor of a former Byzantine church in present-day Madaba, Jordan. It was discovered in 1884 and is now inside the nineteenth-century Church of St. George that was subsequently built over it (the mosaic remains on the sanctuary floor). Full of biblical references, pilgrimage churches, and eschatological resonance, the Madaba Map depicts the Holy Land at the height of its Byzantine glory. It also includes non-Christianized, or secular, features, such as city walls, gates, and streets. Our focus is on the map's image of Jerusalem, which includes *all* of the Circuit's intramural stations, namely, the Holy

Sepulchre, the Church of Holy Sion, Holy Wisdom, and the Church of St. Mary at the pool of the Bethesda. The mosaic also features streets that would have served as pathways: the colonnaded western cardo (the principal street of Jerusalem), the city's eastern cardo (half-colonnaded on the map), and the lane from the eastern cardo to the East Gate.[8] Doing the Jerusalem Circuit today is, in part, an exercise in walking the Madaba Map.

Fig. 2. Jerusalem on the Madaba Map, c. 600. The Church of St. George, Madaba, Jordan. Photo by Dick Osseman. Used with permission.

The Stations

Both in terms of their on-the-ground status and what's recorded in a given text, there are some fluctuations in the stations. In this sense, the *route* of the Circuit is more consistent than the corresponding list of places. While the Circuit always included the Holy Sepulchre, Holy Sion, the Gethsemane area, and the Mount of Olives, at least one site was abandoned and one monument was added over the centuries in question. Just as some sites flourished and some were diminished at times, no one text mentions all of the places and commemorations associated with the Circuit. Still, with some discretion, we know what the stations were.

The Jerusalem Circuit began at the Holy Sepulchre, a complex of chapels, shrines, and courtyards composed of three principal areas: (1) the tomb of Christ housed inside the Anastasis (the "Resurrection"), a large circular structure also known as the Rotunda; (2) the rock of Golgotha, or Calvary, the place of Jesus' crucifixion; and (3) a two-story, double-aisled church, known as the Basilica of Constantine, or the Martyrium (the "Place of Witness"); its apse was identified in the pre-Crusader period as the place

---

8. The street grid of Jerusalem dates to Hadrian's second-century renovation of Jerusalem.

where the Holy Cross was found by Helena (d. 330), the mother of Constantine the Great (d. 337).

The next station was the Church of Holy Sion on the summit of Mount Sion (the Western Hill), reached by walking south on the city's western cardo. Extended to the south in the sixth century, the cardo directly linked the Holy Sepulchre and the Nea Church.[9] From the termination of the cardo, Holy Sion was a couple hundred meters to the southwest. Known as the Mother of All Churches (*mater omnium ecclesiarum*) due to its apostolic associations, Holy Sion had three primary memories: (1) Pentecost and the descent of the Holy Spirit; (2) the Lord's Supper, including Jesus' washing of the disciples' feet; and (3) the death of Mary. The commemorations collectively testified to Mount Sion as the Jerusalem center of the New Testament church.

Pilgrims of the Byzantine period proceeded from Holy Sion to the Church of Holy Wisdom, or Hagia Sophia, which commemorated Jesus' trial before Pilate. Holy Wisdom was destroyed in the Persian conquest of 614 and the church was never rebuilt; the site is not mentioned in the pilgrim texts of the Early Islamic period. Ruins of the church have not been identified; however, from textual accounts, we know that the church was opposite the western wall of the Temple Mount, communicating with—or certainly near—the city's eastern cardo which ran in a north-south direction through the Central, or Tyropoeon, Valley, parallel to the western side of the Temple Mount.[10] Based on the textual evidence, we can identify the church on the Madaba Map.

It's worth emphasizing that during the Byzantine period there was a church specifically dedicated to Jesus' trial before Pilate that was presumed by pilgrims to be the actual house, or praetorium, of Pilate. The church contained Pilate's alleged judgment seat at the Gabbatha pavement (John 19:16) and the column upon which Jesus was scourged. After the destruction of Holy Wisdom, Jesus' trial before Pilate was relocated on Mount Sion near the Church of Holy Sion before being moved once again to the

---

9. On the New Church of Mary the Theotokos (commonly known as the Nea) built by the emperor Justinian (d. 565), see Procopius, *On Buildings* 5.1–5; Schick, *Christian Communities*, 332–33; Murphy-O'Connor, *Holy Land*, 83–84. The Nea church is prominently depicted on the Madaba Map.

10. Hadrian's eastern cardo was approximately ninety meters to the west of the Herodian street that ran along the western side of the Temple Mount; see Magness, *Jerusalem*, 349.

The Jerusalem Circuit

Antonia fortress on the northwest corner of the Temple Mount by the late Crusader period.

Although the Jerusalem Circuit lost an important station after 614, the route through the city remained the same. Post-Byzantine pilgrims (knowingly or not) bypassed the site on their way to the subsequent station, the pool of Bethesda, going around the northwest corner of the Temple Mount. From Holy Sion, pilgrims descended the eastern slope of the Western Hill until they came to the eastern cardo. Turning north (left), they took the eastern cardo past (the former site of) Holy Wisdom, eventually veering east on the street that led to the city's eastern gate. The pool of Bethesda was just inside the East Gate to the north (left) of the road. Both streets—and all three churches—appear on the Madaba Map.

Also known as the Probatica, or the Sheep Pool, the biblical site of Bethesda (Bethzatha) was a double pool separated by a central dike 6.5 meters wide. In the Christian period, the pool of Bethesda was a twinned site with two distinct commemorations. A Byzantine church dedicated to Jesus' healing of the paralytic (John 5) was built on top of the dike with supporting buttresses extending down into the pools below. Christians also placed the birth of Mary at Bethesda, representing a tradition contained in the *Protevangelium of James* (c. 200) that Mary was born in Jerusalem.[11] The church was variously called the Church of the Paralytic and the Church of Mary.

Following the twinned site of Bethesda, the Circuit left the city through the East Gate on its way to Gethsemane in the Jehoshaphat Valley. Just outside the gate, post-Byzantine pilgrims encountered a monument associated with Mary's funeral. According to Jerusalem tradition, after Mary's death on Mount Sion, the apostles carried her body to her tomb at Gethsemane. During the procession, her funeral was interrupted by a Jew traditionally known as Jephonias (some versions describe a group of Jews). When Jephonias tried to steal Mary's body, his hands became stuck to the bier as a sword-bearing angel suddenly appeared, severing his hands from his body. The confrontation ended with Jephonias's conversion to the Christian faith—and the restoration of his hands. A column marking the Jephonias incident was erected in the seventh century outside the East Gate; it's the best example of a monument built along the existing route of the Circuit.

The next station was the Church of Mary's Tomb. Following the Jephonias incident, the funeral procession continued to Gethsemane where

---

11. *Protevangelium of James* 1–5.

Mary was entombed before her body, according to assumptionist traditions, was physically assumed into heaven. The Church of Mary's Tomb was a large round building with two levels: an upper church and a lower church (crypt) containing her tomb.

The Circuit proceeded with the Gethsemane sites associated with Jesus—a natural grotto and a Byzantine church—marking separate events of the same story. The Grotto of Gethsemane, a natural cave only meters away from Mary's tomb, is described in the pilgrim accounts as a place where Jesus and his disciples ate and slept together; it was also the place of Jesus' betrayal and arrest. Uphill from the grotto was the Church of Gethsemane, where Jesus prayed "in agony" before his capture and subsequent execution. Therefore, pilgrims encountered Jesus' arrest before his prayer in the garden.

Leaving Gethsemane, the Circuit climbed the Mount of Olives, an ascent that is noted in the sources. According to *The Armenian Guide*, it was eight hundred steps to the summit, while Sophronius declares: "From that famous valley I will mount those steps, and venerate the Mount of Olives."[12] On the top of the ridge, the Circuit concluded with two final stations: the Eleona and the Church of the Ascension. The Church of the Eleona (meaning "of the Olives") was built over a cave where, according to tradition, Jesus taught his disciples about the end of time, teachings known as the Apocalyptic Discourse that took place during the final days of Jesus' life (Matt 24, Mark 13, Luke 21). Along with the Holy Sepulchre and the Church of the Nativity in Bethlehem, the Eleona was one of the first three Holy Land churches commissioned by Constantine and was an important church throughout the Byzantine period. Although it maintained a Christian presence, the Eleona was a diminished site in the Early Islamic period, especially compared to the adjacent place of Jesus' ascension approximately fifty meters away.

A place of anticipant vigil of Christ's return, the Church of the Ascension kindled the religious imagination of pilgrims. Centered around the last footprints of Christ, the roofless church—which allowed pilgrims to gaze into the skies of Jesus' ascent—was illuminated at night with a brilliant display of lamps. Commencing with Jesus' resurrection, the Jerusalem Circuit culminated with Jesus' ascension and promised return.

Enhancing the eschatological resonance of the summit, the Mount of Olives offered a breathtaking view of Jerusalem. To the east, pilgrims could

---

12. *Armenian Guide* 7; Sophronius, *Anacreontica* 19.1–3.

glimpse the Jordan River Valley with its life-giving waters of baptism. It was the word-picture to the west, however, that commanded the pilgrims' attention. Sophronius exalts in the scenery before him: "let me . . . regard the beauty of the Holy City lying over to the west. How sweet it is to see thy fair beauty, City of God, from the Mount of Olives!"[13] Rising above the Holy City, the Church of the Ascension offered an astonishing perspective of Jerusalem—the Holy Sepulchre and the walls of the city as well as the temple ruins. The reward for pilgrims who completed the Circuit was a view of New Jerusalem in stone: a foursquare city without a temple with the tomb of Christ as its throne (see Rev 21–22).

Following the Mount of Olives, some texts continue to the tomb of Lazarus in Bethany (an easy day trip from Jerusalem) and others proceed to Bethlehem. At some point, pilgrims would eventually travel to these and other locations. But the Jerusalem Circuit properly ended on the summit of the Mount of Olives: at the place of Jesus' ascension overlooking the Holy City. The Jerusalem Circuit was a walk-through of the holy sites that allowed pilgrims to return to their lodgings by the end of the day, only to repeat the experience throughout their sojourn in the city of Christ's death, resurrection, and expectant return.

THE PRINCIPAL TEXTS

Our discussion of the sources will focus on four texts, which we will simply refer to as Sophronius, *The Armenian Guide*, Willibald, and Bernard. The date of the Jerusalem material and the language of the texts are as follows:

- Sophronius (before 614): Greek
- *The Armenian Guide* (c. 630): Armenian
- Willibald (724–26): Latin
- Bernard (870): Latin

Maps charting the order of the Jerusalem material make the visual case for the Circuit. Note: the arrows indicate the sequence of the sites not the pathways on the ground.

---

13. Sophronius, *Anacreontica* 19.13–18.

Walking the Jerusalem Circuit

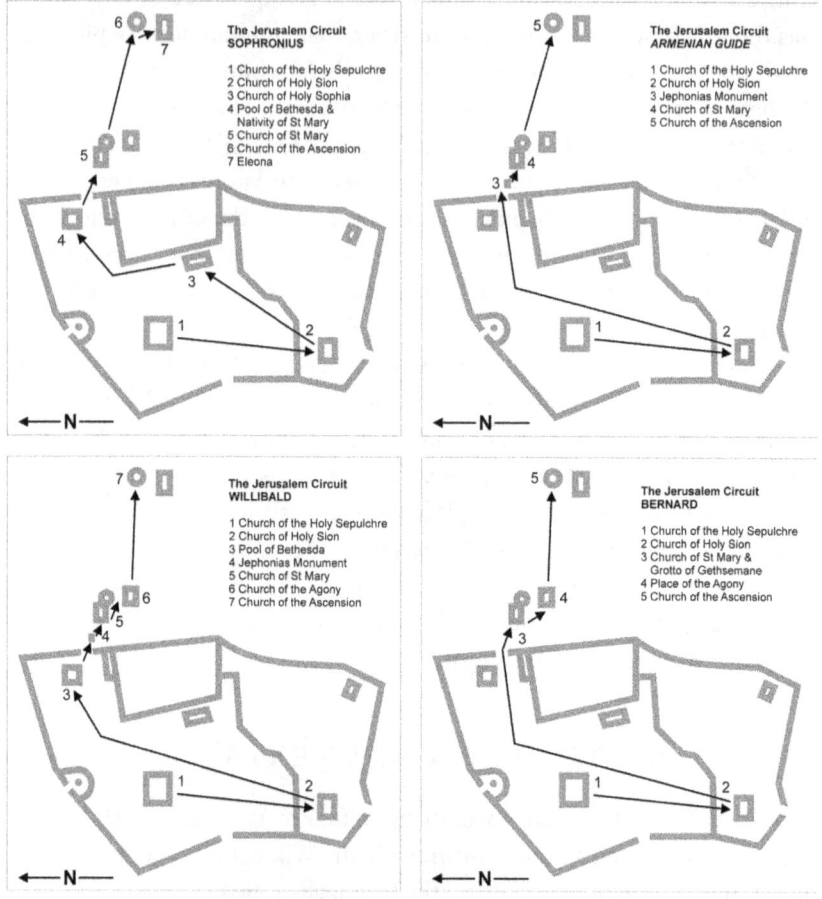

Fig. 3. The Jerusalem Circuit: Four Principal Texts.

Sophronius (before 614)

Sophronius of Jerusalem (c. 560–c. 638) lived twice in the Holy City: first as a monk at the monastery of St. Theodosius beginning around the year 580 and later as the patriarch of Jerusalem in 634 after spending a number of years in Egypt. Sophronius was the Christian patriarch at the time of the Arab conquest in 638, famously handing over the keys of the city to Caliph 'Umar. The date of his death is uncertain but occurred shortly after the Muslim takeover of Jerusalem.

Sophronius wrote metered verse known as *anacreontica*, some of which were written while he was absent from Jerusalem expressing a longing to return to the holy places. Poems 19 and 20 appear to be in the wrong order. *Anacreonticon* 19, which begins at the foot of the Mount of Olives, opens like the continuation of a previous poem, and scholars have shown that their order should be reversed and connected as a whole. The texts describe the Christian topography of Jerusalem prior to the Persian conquest of 614.

Sophronius begins by standing at the gates of the Holy City before walking to the Holy Sepulchre. There, he commences with the Anastasis—the place of Jesus' resurrection—where "the King of All rose again, trampling down the power of death." He gazes at the stone that sealed the tomb, now in the form of a cube, before entering the divine sanctuary of Jesus' tomb. Sophronius then proceeds to the Place of the Skull (Golgotha), which he identifies as the navel of the world, before coming to the Basilica of Constantine where Helena found the Holy Cross. He mentions the relic of the True Cross and the reed, the sponge, and the lance of the crucifixion.

Speeding on, Sophronius continues to the Church of Holy Sion, referencing Pentecost and the descent of the Holy Spirit, the Lord's Supper and Jesus' washing of the disciples' feet, the death of Mary, and the resurrection appearance of Jesus. Leaving the summit of Mount Sion, Sophronius goes to the Church of Holy Wisdom, the place of Jesus' trial before Pilate, where a stone marks the place where Jesus was scourged. He then visits the twinned site of the pool of Bethesda and the birthplace of Mary: "the holy Probatica, where the all-renowned Anna bore Mary."

The text then moves to Gethsemane to the Church of Mary's Tomb. Sophronius mentions Gethsemane in relation to Mary but does not refer to the Gethsemane commemorations of Jesus: neither the grotto nor the church of Jesus' prayer. Although the omission is noteworthy, any reference to Gethsemane would recall to readers Jesus' agony, betrayal, and arrest.

Anacreontica 20 ends by praising the lofty mountain from where Jesus looked into heaven, an allusion to Jesus' ascension. The beginning of *Anacreontica* 19 begins with the climb: leaving Gethsemane, Sophronius mounts the steps to the top of the Mount of Olives where the Lord ascended, visiting the Ascension church before the Eleona, where Jesus "taught the divine mysteries" of the end times "shedding light into secret depths." Although the Sophronius text differs slightly from the notion that the Circuit ended at the Church of the Ascension, the Eleona was eclipsed by the latter in the Early Islamic period. To be sure, the eschatological focus of the neighboring sites complemented one another; their locations and end-of-time focus were essentially the same.

What the Sophronius text uniquely provides is a poignant pause at the top: a first-person testimony of the view from the Mount of Olives looking back over the city of Jerusalem: "Then let me go out through the Great Doors [of the Eleona] onto the steps, and regard the beauty of the Holy City lying over to the west. How sweet it is to see thy fair beauty, City of God, from the Mount of Olives!" While the text continues with descriptions of Bethany and Bethlehem, the dramatic pause on the summit of the Mount of Olives—the breathtaking panorama of the Holy City—culminates the Jerusalem material.

The Armenian Guide (c. 630)

The Armenian Guide can be securely dated after the Persian conquest of 614: the Church of Holy Wisdom is not mentioned, while Jesus' trial before Pilate is located on Mount Sion. It also appears to predate the Arab conquest of 638 as there is no sense of Muslim control of the city, let alone development of the Haram esh-Sharif (the former Temple Mount), which places the text in the Interconquest period (614–38). Since the Jephonias monument (station 11) was likely built in the wake of Heraclius's restoration of the True Cross in 630, we'll date the text accordingly.

A brief text, *The Armenian Guide* is an example of an impersonal guide that was used by actual pilgrims who walked the sites. As well as moving the reader through the city using cardinal directions (north, south), relative directions (left, right), and distances, it also refers to steps and paces.

The Jerusalem Circuit of *The Armenian Guide* consists of the following stations:

- the Holy Sepulchre,
- Holy Sion and surroundings,
- the Jephonias monument,
- Mary's tomb, and
- the Church of the Ascension.

The Armenian Guide begins with the Holy Sepulchre, describing its three major areas: the tomb of Christ and the Anastasis, the Martyrium (the

The Jerusalem Circuit

Basilica of Constantine) containing the place where the Holy Cross was found, and the Church of Golgotha with the place of the crucifixion above the tomb of Adam. Relics include the spear, the sponge, and the chalice of the Last Supper.

The Armenian Guide then moves to the Church of Holy Sion, which housed the crown of thorns. Of the church's three primary commemorations, only the Last Supper is mentioned. References to Pentecost and the death of Mary are not included.

As previously noted, the Church of Holy Wisdom, destroyed in 614, is omitted from the text. The palace of Pilate called Gabbatha—and with it the footprints of the Lord where he stood before Pilate—is now located to the "right" of Holy Sion. Nearby is the prison of Christ, also associated with Jesus' trial. Although it is not mentioned in *The Armenian Guide*, the Byzantine house of Caiaphas was near Holy Sion, understood to be the site of the present-day Armenian monastery of St. Savior immediately outside Sion Gate. Moving the Pilate commemoration to Mount Sion placed both of Jesus' trials in the same vicinity.

While we can account for the relocation of Jesus' trial before Pilate, more inexplicably, *The Armenian Guide* mentions neither the pool of Bethesda nor the birthplace of Mary, even though the twinned site remained important in the post-Byzantine period as mentioned by Willibald and the *Commemoratorium* (c. 808).[14]

Instead, the next site after Mount Sion is the Jephonias monument which was just outside the East Gate overlooking the Jehoshaphat Valley. Given the location of the monument—its elevation above the valley is important—the text assumes a route that exits the city through the East Gate. In other words, rather than walking around the southeast corner of the Temple Mount, up the Jehoshaphat Valley, and climbing back up to the East Gate, the text implicitly takes pilgrims through the city, passing the ruins of Holy Wisdom and the pool of Bethesda along the way. It is assumed, moreover, that the Jephonias column was intentionally placed along the route of the Circuit.

From the Jephonias monument, there was a descent of 250 steps to the tomb of Mary in the Gethsemane Valley. While Gethsemane is mentioned, once again, Jesus' association with the place—his prayer, betrayal, and arrest—is omitted. From the tomb of Mary, 800 steps led up the Mount of Olives to a beautiful circular church that marked the place of Jesus' ascension.

---

14. See Hugeburc, *Life of Willibald* 19; *Commemoratorium* 8.

The Eleona is not included. Despite omitting some key stations and commemorations, *The Armenian Guide* charts the same route as Sophronius and the later texts of Willibald and Bernard.

Willibald (724–26)

A century after Sophronius and *The Armenian Guide*, the Willibald text reflects the state of Christian pilgrimage some ninety years into Muslim rule following the Arab conquest of 638: as evidenced by the text, the Circuit was formative to the experience—and memories—of Christian pilgrims in the Early Islamic period.

Born in 700 in Anglo-Saxon England, Willibald stayed in Jerusalem on four occasions during his visit to the Holy Land (724–26). Over fifty years later at the age of seventy-eight, Willibald, now the bishop of Eichstätt in present-day Germany, dictated his life and travels to the nun Hugeburc, who composed the text. In describing the sites of the Holy City, Willibald follows the template of the Jerusalem Circuit. Remarkably, only stations of the Circuit are included; not a single site is mentioned that is off the route. Even if Willibald consulted written notes of his travels (there is no evidence that he did), the point remains: Willibald's Jerusalem experience, including his long-term memories, was fundamentally shaped by the Circuit. As extraordinary as it seems, it appears that Willibald was so familiar with the Circuit—that it was so firmly etched in his memory from walking it numerous times—that he could accurately order the sites using the Circuit as a mnemonic device a half century after his travels.

Willibald's circuit of Jerusalem consists of now familiar stations:

- the Holy Sepulchre, including the place where the Holy Cross was found, the place of Calvary, and the tomb of Christ;
- the Church of Holy Sion, where Mary died (neither Pentecost nor the Last Supper is mentioned);
- the pool of Bethesda, where the Lord cured a paralytic (Mary's birth is not mentioned);
- the Jephonias monument, where a Jew tried to seize Mary's body;
- the Church of Mary's Tomb;

The Jerusalem Circuit

- the Church of Gethsemane, where the Lord prayed before his passion (the grotto is not mentioned);[15] and
- the Church of the Ascension, where the Lord ascended into heaven (the Eleona is not included).

The location of Willibald's Jephonias monument ("a great column") has been previously misidentified—it has been associated with the North Gate column of the Madaba Map as well as the South Gate on Mount Sion—which has obscured recognition that the text adheres to the Jerusalem Circuit. Located outside the East Gate, it is the same monument described by *The Armenian Guide* and Epiphanius as a structure with four columns. The apparent discrepancy in the monument's appearance is resolved by the fact that the monument of the miraculous healing at the Holy Sepulchre is likewise described as a giant column by a Latin text and as a four-columned structure in a Greek one.[16]

We have previously noted that Willibald's account of Jerusalem is presented as a walk through the city. Highlighting language from the text (Hugeburc changes Willibald's dictations to the third person), Willibald moves from site to site as follows:

> From the Holy Sepulchre, Willibald set off (*abiit*) for the Church of Holy Sion. He then went (*ibat*) to the pool of the paralytic healing. Outside the East Gate was the Jephonias monument. Descending from there (*inde discendens*), Willibald came (*venit*) to the Valley of Jehoshaphat and the Church of St. Mary. From there, he ascended (*ascendit*) to the Church in Gethsemane where the Lord prayed before he came (*venit*) to the Church of the Ascension.

There is one wrinkle in Willibald's account. He visits the Holy Sepulchre upon arriving in Jerusalem on the feast of St. Martin (November 11, 724). He then falls ill, staying in bed until a week before Christmas, when, feeling stronger, he sets off for Holy Sion and the remaining sites of Jerusalem. In other words, the text presents Willibald visiting the Holy Sepulchre on one day and completing the Circuit beginning with Holy Sion on another day a month later. We should assume that Willibald revisited—and started from—the Holy Sepulchre before proceeding to Holy Sion. However, as the text had already described the Holy Sepulchre, it is not mentioned again.

15. On Willibald's church of Jesus' prayer, see station 14.
16. See Aist, *Christian Topography*, 166–74, including maps 8–10.

The temporal break caused by Willibald's illness underscores an important distinction between the Holy Sepulchre and rest of the Circuit. As the place of Jesus' death and resurrection, the Holy Sepulchre was a destinational center of its own, and on a given day, pilgrims would have visited the complex without necessarily continuing to other sites, let alone completing the Circuit. Similarly, pilgrims walked the Circuit multiple times during their sojourn in the city, but presumably not as often as they visited the Holy Sepulchre.

It is also the case that Willibald's descriptions, though meager in places, represent his collective memory of the sites over repeated visits, including multiple iterations of the Circuit during his four sojourns in the city. The only reference to a repeated visit occurs at the beginning of Willibald's second sojourn when, following a temporary bout of blindness contracted while visiting sites south of Jerusalem, he is healed upon entering the church where the Holy Cross was found. Denoting the entrance to the Basilica of Constantine at the eastern end of the Holy Sepulchre, this is likely an implicit reference to the monument of the miraculous healing associated with the legend of the Holy Cross.[17] Finally, while they are not mentioned in the text, Willibald presumably visited other sites that were not on the route, such as Aceldama and the pool of Siloam.[18]

Bernard the Monk (870)

Born in France, Bernard the Monk visited Jerusalem in 870. The last full pilgrimage account prior to the Crusades, the text contains the earliest description of the liturgy of the Holy Fire.[19] Bernard's circuit begins with the Holy Sepulchre—the tomb of Christ, Calvary, the Basilica of Constantine with the place of the Holy Cross, and the center of the world—before proceeding to churches on Mount Sion that commemorate the Last Supper, the death of Mary, the stoning of Stephen, and Peter's denial of Jesus. Bernard mentions the former Temple Mount, now containing a mosque, as well as gates associated with Peter's imprisonment. Although these sites were off the route, they can be accounted for as observations of a pilgrim walking

---

17. See Aist, *Christian Topography*, 63–106; Adomnán, *On the Holy Places* 1.11 (see station 4).

18. For pilgrims who did, see Adomnán, *On the Holy Places* 1.19 (Aceldama); Bernard the Monk, *Journey to the Holy Places* 16 (pool of Siloam).

19. Bernard the Monk, *Journey to the Holy Places* 11.

the Circuit—namely, places that Bernard could see as he descended the eastern slope of Mount Sion toward the eastern cardo. Tellingly, Bernard locates these extra-Circuit sites with directional language—to the north and south of Holy Sion—rather than using words of physical movement: they don't appear to have been directly a part of his walk.

Bernard's account continues by "going outside Jerusalem" and down to Gethsemane in the Jehoshaphat Valley. While the pool of Bethesda is not mentioned, his *descent* to Gethsemane *after* he left the city indicates that he's taking the same route as the previous texts—from Mount Sion he went around the northwest corner of the Temple Mount exiting out the East Gate rather than coming *up* the Jehoshaphat Valley. Bernard next mentions the Church of Mary's Tomb and the church where Jesus was betrayed, containing four round tables where Jesus ate with his disciples: a reference to the Grotto of Gethsemane. From there, Bernard hurried to the lower slopes of the Mount of Olives, where he visited the place of Jesus' prayer (no church is mentioned). Citing a minor commemoration on the mountain side, Bernard notes the place where the Pharisees brought the adulterous woman to Jesus, marked by a church containing a rock with the words that Jesus wrote on the ground (John 8:1–11). Bernard then climbed the Mount of Olives to the Church of the Ascension. The Eleona, once again, is not included.

In sum, Bernard's account follows the same route as the other texts. Although his description includes some minor commemorations, the principal stations appear in their expected order: the Holy Sepulchre, Holy Sion, the Church of Mary's Tomb, the Grotto of Gethsemane, Jesus' agony, and the Church of the Ascension. Notably, Bernard's later reference to the pool of Siloam occurs after he returns from Bethany: he eventually visited the Siloam pool and included it in his overall account of the city, but it was not a part of his initial description of the holy sites. Due to the direction the Circuit took around the Temple Mount, the pool of Siloam had long become a secondary site. Shaping Bernard's experience of the Holy City, the text's primary Jerusalem material is structured according to the Circuit.

CRUSADER CHANGES

In the pilgrimage texts of the Crusader period, the order of the material changes. The primary difference is due to Crusade interest in the Temple Mount. Unlike their Byzantine counterparts, who neglected the site seeing the temple ruins as a visible fulfillment of Jesus' prophecy, the Crusaders, captured by the mystique of King Solomon, utilized the space that had been developed by Muslims during the Early Islamic period (the Haram esh-Sharif). The Crusaders referred to the Dome of the Rock as the Temple of the Lord and the al-Aqsa Mosque (al-Jami' al-Aqsa) as the Temple of Solomon. The Dome of the Rock was used as a church; the latter functioned as a royal palace before being given to the Knights Templar, whose name derives from their use of the site. Crusader sources generally describe the sites on the Temple Mount following their account of the Holy Sepulchre, while the placement of Holy Sion (previously second) no longer occurs in a particular order. Since our interest is on the pre-Crusader Circuit, it is sufficient to note that with Crusader interest in the Temple Mount pilgrim movement through the city changed along with the texts.

THE STATUS QUO

Today, four sites on the Circuit—the Holy Sepulchre, the Cenacle, the Church of Mary's Tomb, and the Chapel of the Ascension—are part of the Status Quo arrangement which regulates the use and possession of certain sites between Christian denominations and the Abrahamic faiths. The arrangement stems from the Ottoman period, and subsequent authorities—the British, Jordanian, and Israeli governments—have recognized the Status Quo, although not always without complications. The Status Quo is also affirmed in the Fundamental Agreement between Israel and the Vatican signed in Jerusalem on December 30, 1993.[20]

To summarize how the Status Quo developed, after the Ottomans took over Constantinople in 1453, they proclaimed the Greek patriarch of Constantinople the religious and civil authority for all Christians residing in the Ottoman Empire. In 1516, when the Ottoman Empire gained control of Jerusalem, the balance of power with respect to the holy places changed accordingly: the Greek Orthodox presence was strengthened at the expense of Franciscan interests.

In 1757, when Sultan Mustafa III (d. 1774) gave the Greeks the Church of Mary's Tomb and the Church of the Nativity in Bethlehem, along with co-equal rights in the Holy Sepulchre, clashes broke out between the groups. In reply to the French ambassador's objections, the grand vizier replied: "These places belong to my lord the Sultan. He gives them to whomever he

---

20. Available online at: https://www.vatican.va/roman_curia/secretariat_state/archivio/documents/rc_seg-st_19931230_santa-sede-israele_en.html.

pleases. They may have always been owned by the Franciscans, but now His Highness wants them to belong to the Greeks."

Vested interest in the holy places extended well beyond Jerusalem: at the time, the Russian tsar was the protector of Orthodox interests, while France assumed the role for Catholics. After the 1808 fire in the Holy Sepulchre, the Greeks further consolidated their position, and subsequent attempts to reverse the gains were largely unsuccessful. The situation came to a head in the Crimean War (1853–54), with the dispute over the holy sites a contributing cause of the conflict.

Just prior to the war—in February 1852 and again in May 1853—the Sultan Abdülmecid I published a *firman*, or royal degree, which effectively established the Status Quo (Latin for "the state in which things are"), though it simply declared that everything would be left as it was: "The actual status quo will be maintained and the Jerusalem shrines, whether owned in common or exclusively by the Greek, Latin, and Armenian communities, will all remain forever in their present state."[21] At the end of the war, the Status Quo was recognized in the Treaty of Paris (1856) and later in the Treaty of Berlin (1878).

Though acknowledged in treaties, the Status Quo arrangement was never officially written down. The most pertinent document is *The Status Quo in the Holy Places* written by L. G. A. Cust in 1929 for the British Mandate Government. Cust's report is considered an authoritative source on the Status Quo and is used today by the Israeli authorities.[22]

Since the Status Quo stems from the Ottoman period, the laws regulating the sites are based on Muslim, or sharia, law. The most important concept is the waqf: a holy place of any religion is an inalienable religious endowment that has no absolute title; no one owns it. The Status Quo also adheres to Ottoman property law. Relevant examples include: payment for the repair of a structure indicates possession, and the owner of the covering of a building owns the building. One of the important distinctions of the Status Quo is between *rights of possession* and *rights of usage*. A group may possess a space, though no one actually owns it. Alternatively, a community may have limited rights of usage for liturgical purposes but not possess the space where the liturgy takes place.

---

21. Quoted in Cohen, *Saving the Holy Sepulchre*, 8.

22. The Cust text can be found online. See, for instance, the website of the Economic Cooperation Foundation: https://ecf.org.il/issues/issue/1413.

The Status Quo applies to nearly a dozen sites, and a few, like the Cenacle, have been added to the list that appears in the Cust report. Public attention tends to focus on the Holy Sepulchre; the arrangement regulates the building's use among six Christian traditions: three major communities (Greek Orthodox, Franciscan, and Armenian Orthodox) and three minor communities (Syrian Orthodox, Coptic, and Ethiopian).[23] Some of the spaces are held in common. A color-coded map of the Holy Sepulchre identifying the areas of the complex according to community can be found online.

A CONTEMPORARY PRAYER WALK

Traditionally, Holy Land pilgrims have been interested in the Jerusalem of their day, and an important dimension of walking the Circuit is engaging the contemporary city: recognizing commonalities and differences among its residents, religious communities, and pilgrim visitors, observing people and interacting with others, and praying for the peace of the city. A brief survey of the sites highlights the rich tapestry of religious communities and national interests that comprise the contemporary iteration of the Jerusalem Circuit:

- four Status Quo sites: the Holy Sepulchre, the Cenacle, the Church of Mary's Tomb, and the Chapel of the Ascension;
- sites used by six Christian churches: Greek Orthodox, Roman Catholic, Armenian Orthodox, Syrian Orthodox, Coptic, and Ethiopian;
- four Catholic communities: the Franciscans, the Benedictines, the White Fathers, and the Carmelite Sisters;
- two original Constantinian foundations: the Holy Sepulchre and the Eleona;
- two sites that are French national properties: St. Anne's and the Eleona;
- an Antonio Barluzzi church: the Basilica of Gethsemane;[24]
- a Muslim site: the Chapel of the Ascension;

---

23. See Cohen, *Saving the Holy Sepulchre*.
24. The Franciscan Antonio Barluzzi (d. 1960), the "modern architect" of the holy land, designed and restored twenty-four churches and hospitals between 1912 and 1955.

- four sites that have either been a mosque or an Islamic school, not counting the Holy Sepulchre whose keys are kept by Muslim families: the Cenacle, the Church of St. Anne, the Church of Mary's Tomb, and the Chapel of the Ascension;
- a site that is the administrative possession of the Israeli Ministry of Interior: the Cenacle; and
- two stations that are no longer extant: Holy Wisdom and the Jephonias monument (surrogate locations are a Jewish holy site and a Muslim cemetery).

The stations contain Roman, Byzantine, Crusader, and Muslim archaeology, modern art and mosaics, tombs and grottoes, olive gardens and overlooks.

This doesn't begin to take in the treasures along the route, which traverses the Christian, Jewish, and Muslim quarters and skirts the Armenian area. It goes by Jewish holy sites (e.g., the Hurva Synagogue, the tomb of David, the Western Wall Plaza), provides views of the Dome of the Rock and the al-Aqsa Mosque, proceeds through streets of Mamluk and Ottoman architecture, and passes additional synagogues, mosques, and churches, including stations of the Via Dolorosa. The Circuit offers vistas of the city walls and the valleys surrounding Jerusalem, as well as broad panoramas of skylines, horizons, and distant mountains, including the separation barrier and the kingdom of Jordan. One sees children, monks, and soldiers, the privileged and the oppressed. As with most things in Jerusalem, the route is contextually rich and layered, at times overwhelming. While commemorating Christian sites, the Jerusalem Circuit is an open-eyed journey through the City of God, a place diverse and divided, both beautiful and scarred, where heaven intermingles with earth, and earth descends to the depths of Hades, a reference to Jerusalem's Hinnom Valley, linked in biblical tradition with hell (e.g., Mark 9:43–48). With both the temple and the Holy Sepulchre associated with heaven, the physical topography of Jerusalem encompasses the cosmos of God's creation as well as the spiritual spectrum of the human condition. Encountering a city full of tensions, contradictions, and paradox, the ancient practice of the pilgrim Circuit offers itself as a contemporary prayer walk for the peace of Jerusalem.

2.

Practicalities and Logistics

Fig. 4. *Hierosolima*, 1493. Michael Wolgemut (German, 1434–1519). An imaginary representation of the temple in the middle of walled Jerusalem. In Hartmann Schedel, *Liber chronicarum*, published in Nuremburg by Anton Koberger. Woodcut. Amir Cahanovitc Collection. The National Library of Israel. Public domain.

Practicalities and Logistics

WALKING THE CIRCUIT

The Jerusalem Circuit is approximately four kilometers, or 2.5 miles, including five hundred steps up the Mount of Olives. Allowing for sufficient time at each station, the Circuit takes between 4.5 to six hours to complete; the walk alone is between one and 1.5 hours. The Circuit can be done as an all-day exercise with a planned lunch break, completed in half a day—either in the morning or afternoon—or walked in sections over multiple days.

Recommended: The All-Day Option (8:00–17:00)

The full-day experience allows for a leisurely pace, extended time at the sites, and more interactions with others. Commence with the Holy Sepulchre between 7:30–8:00, departing for Holy Sion by 8:45. After commemorating the stations of Holy Sion, take a break at the Dormition Abbey café. Continue no later than 10:30, stopping at the Western Wall Plaza to commemorate the former Church of Holy Wisdom. Arrive at St. Anne's at least by 11:15, which closes at 12:00. Enjoy lunch in the Old City or proceed to Gethsemane for a picnic lunch. Continuing with the remaining stations in the afternoon, aim to be at the Chapel of the Ascension by 16:30. Note that it gets dark in the winter before 17:00.

The key to the all-day option is navigating the midday closures of St. Anne's, the tomb of Mary, and the Grotto of Gethsemane. The three Gethsemane sites can be done in any order to most efficiently manage the lunch break.

- The Church of St. Anne: closed 12:00–14:00
- The Church of Mary's Tomb: closed 12:30–14:00
- The Grotto of Gethsemane: closed 12:00–14:30
- The Church of Gethsemane: open all day

This leaves the following options:

- **A lunch break between 12:00–14:00.** Finish the stations at St. Anne's by 12:00 when the site closes. You'll have a two-hour break until the tomb of Mary opens at 14:00. This option works well with a sit-down lunch in the Old City.

- **A lunch break between 12:30–14:30.** Finish the tomb of Mary at 12:30 when the site closes (remember the previous site, St. Anne's, closes at 12:00). You'll have a two-hour break until the adjacent site, the Grotto of Gethsemane, opens at 14:30. This option works best with a picnic lunch in the Gethsemane area. To shorten the lunch break, visit the Church of Gethsemane before the grotto reopens.
- **No set lunch break.** Provided that you finish the stations of St. Anne's and the Grotto of Gethsemane by 12:00—and the tomb of Mary by 12:30—you can proceed to the Church of Gethsemane, which stays open all day. This is more easily done by switching the order of the tomb of Mary and the Grotto of Gethsemane. The subsequent site, the Eleona, reopens at 14:00.

The Morning Option (7:30–12:30)

The Holy Sepulchre opens very early in the morning; however, the Dormition Abbey (station 7) does not open until 9:00. Commence with the stations of the Holy Sepulchre no later than 7:30. Leave the Holy Sepulchre at 8:15, arriving at the Cenacle around 8:30 (it opens at 8:00); visit the Dormition Abbey beginning at 9:00. That leaves approximately two and a half hours (9:30–12:00) to visit St. Anne's, the three Gethsemane sites, and the Eleona, as well as commemorating Holy Wisdom and the Jephonias monument along the way, before the Eleona closes at noon (last entry 11:45). The final station, the Chapel of the Ascension, is open throughout the day, allowing the Circuit to be finished around 12:30. End with lunch overlooking the city either with a picnic or at the rooftop café across the street.

The Afternoon Option (11:30–17:00)

To walk the Circuit in the afternoon, start between 11:30–12:00 with the Holy Sepulchre, continuing with Holy Sion and Holy Wisdom in time to arrive at St. Anne's at 14:00 when it reopens after lunch. By the time you visit St. Anne's and proceed to Gethsemane, the other sites have reopened for the afternoon. The final station, the Ascension chapel, closes at 17:00, giving approximately 2.5 hours (14:30–17:00) to visit the remaining stations after leaving St. Anne's. Remember that it gets dark in the winter before 17:00. For lunch, eat before commencing the Circuit or grab something quick along the way prior to St. Anne's. Again, the key to the afternoon Circuit is being at St. Anne's when it reopens at 14:00.

The Two-Day Option

The Circuit can also be done in two mornings or two afternoons.

- Day 1 (8:00–12:00 *or* 12:00–17:00): the Holy Sepulchre to St. Anne's
- Day 2 (8:00–12:00 *or* 14:00–17:00): the Gethsemane sites to the Mount of Olives[1]

The Route

Although most people walking the Circuit will know their way around the city or will simply follow their phones, pay attention to the book's station-by-station written directions. For instance, while there is more than one way to walk from the Holy Sepulchre to Holy Sion, follow the western cardo, which was the pilgrim way between the churches. Helpful city maps are posted at several locations on the route; also look over the Jerusalem Circuit of the principal texts, the Byzantine plan of Jerusalem, and the Madaba Map (figs. 1, 3, 5).

Time at the Sites

Below are suggested amounts of time to spend at each site, totaling three to 4.5 hours, excluding the walk. Note: the half-day options must be completed in approximately five hours.

> The Holy Sepulchre: 30–45 minutes
> The Cenacle: 10–15 minutes
> The Dormition Abbey: 15–30 minutes
> Holy Wisdom / the Western Wall Plaza: 10–15 minutes
> The Church of St. Anne / the pool of Bethesda: 25–40 minutes
> The Jephonias Monument / the Muslim cemetery: 5–10 minutes
> The Church of Mary's Tomb: 15–20 minutes
> The Grotto of Gethsemane: 10–15 minutes

---

1. In the afternoon, begin at 14:00 with the Church of Gethsemane before visiting the Grotto of Gethsemane and Church of Mary's Tomb.

The Church of Gethsemane: 20–30 minutes
The Eleona: 25–30 minutes
The Chapel of the Ascension: 15–20 minutes

Total Time at the Stations: 3–4.5 hours
Walking Time: 1–1.5 hours
Total Time: 4–6 hours

Days of the Week

Mondays through Thursdays are the best days to walk the Circuit. Fridays are not recommended as the Old City is crowded and often tense due to Muslim noonday prayers. Traffic in the Jehoshaphat Valley can also be heavy on Fridays. The Franciscan procession of the Stations of the Cross adds to the afternoon crowds. Early Friday morning is manageable, but avoid Fridays if possible. All of the stations are open on Saturday, although Shabbat affects the area around the Cenacle and the Western Wall Plaza. Photography, for instance, is not allowed in the Western Wall Plaza on Shabbat. Although the route can be walked, the stations cannot be completed on Sundays as the Church of St. Anne and the Eleona are closed; the Dormition Abbey is also closed on Sunday mornings.

Opening Hours

Although opening times are provided for each station, it is important to double-check as hours can change. See "Opening Hours" on the Christian Information Center website (www.cicts.org). Once again, be aware of sites that close for lunch, namely, St. Anne's, the Church of Mary's Tomb, the Grotto of Gethsemane, and the Eleona. Also note Sunday closures for Christian sites. Check winter and summer hours, and avoid Yom Kippur, Christmas Day, and New Year when certain stations are closed. Old City access, conditions, and crowds may also be affected by Ramadan, Easter, and other holidays and events.

Admission

There is an admission fee for three sites: St. Anne's (12 NIS / students 10 NIS), the Eleona (10 NIS / students 8 NIS), and the Chapel of the Ascension

(10 NIS). Prices are subject to change. There is no fee for the Holy Sepulchre, the Cenacle, the Dormition Abbey, the Church of Mary's Tomb, the Grotto of Gethsemane, and the Church of Gethsemane.

Dress Code

The dress code for all sites is loose clothing down to the ankles (long trousers, skirts, or dresses) and covered shoulders. Scarves may be used to cover shoulders inside churches.

FOOD, TRANSPORTATION, AND CONVENIENCES

Cafés and kiosks sell water, juice, and snacks along the route. Have sufficient water with you upon leaving the Old City for the Mount of Olives, especially in the summer. There are cafés and convenient stores on the top of the Mount of Olives at the end of the Circuit.

Restaurants and Cafés

Along with the numerous food options on el-Wad Street, we recommend the following cafés and guesthouses that are directly on the route:

- The Dormition Abbey Café (station 7). Coffee and cakes.
- The Austrian Hospice (between stations 8 and 9). Light lunches are available.
- The Ecce Homo Guesthouse (between stations 8 and 9). Lunch only. It is essential to book ahead for the 12:30 lunch.

At the end of the Circuit, enjoy the rooftop café across the street from the Ascension chapel which has a commanding view of the city.

Picnic Lunch

While there are no designated picnic grounds, there are places to sit for a sack lunch in the Jehoshaphat Valley near the Gethsemane sites and on the top of the Mount of Olives. Have plenty of water with you.

Toilets

There are a number of free public toilets in the Old City, some directly on the route, including a large facility at the Western Wall Plaza. Toilets at the sites include: the Holy Sepulchre (free toilets), the Cenacle (free toilets nearby), Dormition Abbey (pay toilets downstairs), St. Anne's (free toilets upon entry), and the Eleona (free toilets upon entry). For the Gethsemane sites, there is a free municipal toilet at the Mount of Olives Information Center on Jericho Road just past the Gethsemane church (a pay toilet on al-Mansourieh Street is sometimes open). On the top of the Mount of Olives, there are free public toilets not far from the Ascension chapel (ask for directions).

Transportation

Transportation up the Mount of Olives can generally be arranged on the spot: there is a taxi stand on Jericho Road across from the Church of Gethsemane. If returning to Jerusalem by foot from the Mount of Olives, avoid al-Mansourieh Street as the narrow road is busy with traffic and doesn't have sidewalks.

General Costs

There is a minimum cost to walking the Circuit, including admission fees at St. Anne's, the Eleona, and the Chapel of the Ascension. Include money for water, snacks, and possibly lunch along the way. Although shopping while walking the Circuit is discouraged, one may wish to purchase a representative souvenir of the experience. Factor in the cost of taxis as needed. Most purchases require Israeli shekels.

SAFETY AND PRECAUTIONS

Ambulance Services

The national emergency number for an ambulance in Israel is 101. The number is answered by Magen David Adom (MDA) around the clock.

Practicalities and Logistics

Passports and Documents

Israeli law requires a person to be able to identify themselves on the spot with official documents. This means carrying one's passport and visa or at the very least photos of them. Identifying documents are particularly important for medical emergencies.

Water

Have sufficient water with you, especially in the summer and before the ascent up the Mount of Olives. Water bottles can be refilled, among other places, in the Western Wall Plaza. Water can be bought along the route in the Old City, Gethsemane, and on the top of the Mount of Olives.

Sun Protection

Wear hats and use sun protection as needed. It can be wise to wear long sleeves and cover necks and feet from the sun in the summer.

Shoes

The entirety of the route is on stone, concrete, or tarmac pavement. Non-slip shoes are essential as pavement stones can be slick in both wet and dry conditions.

Walking Sticks

The route, in places, is steep, uneven, and full of steps. Walking sticks are appropriate for the walk.

Tensions in the City

Although the Old City and the Mount of Olives are safe with person-to-person violent crime essentially unheard of, Jerusalem, of course, is full of political tension. Walk away from the first signs of possible confrontations between Israelis (police, soldiers, or civilians) and Palestinians. The Circuit is not recommended on Fridays as the Old City is crowded due to Muslim noonday prayers at al-Aqsa. Acts of abuse occasionally target Christians (e.g., spitting). While such incidents are important to document and report, if possible, continue with the Circuit without further provoking the situation.

Pickpockets

The vast majority of street vendors are honest people trying to make a living; there is, however, a problem with pickpockets around certain sites, including the Mount of Olives. The sham occurs under the guise of a "vendor" who pretends to be selling a wide item—generally a horizontal photo of Jerusalem—which he cradles in his arms leaving his hands free beneath his wares. Approaching the potential victim head on (face-to-face), the vendor makes bodily contact, furtively removing items such as phones and wallets from the victim's front pockets (men are often targeted). Once you are aware of the technique, it's easy to spot and prevent, even more so if group members are looking out for each other. You should not allow an apparent vendor—especially one holding a horizontal picture of Jerusalem—to make frontal contact with you, and if one does, shouting, turning around, and/or walking away is sufficient to thwart the attempt. If you catch a pickpocket red-handed, confronting or chasing him will often cause him to drop what he took as he wants nothing to do with the police. As a precaution, pilgrims should avoid putting items in front external pockets of shirts and vests, including ones with zippers, and should not wear external money belts (yet, still be careful with back pockets and backpacks). Internal jacket pockets, pockets inside handbags, and trousers with tight front pockets are best. Along with limiting the amount of cash and credit cards you have with you, distribute your valuables placing money, phones, and documents in more than one pocket.

REMEMBERING THE EXPERIENCE

Photos and Videos

The medieval circuit of Jerusalem was a devotional encounter between pilgrims, places, and events of the Christian faith, and you are encouraged to approach the practice in a similar spirit. This begins by immersing yourself in the setting, embodying the experience as an open-eyed exercise that engages the senses. Yet, if a balance can be struck between unmediated perceptions and seeing through a lens, modern technology can enhance one's involvement both during and after the walk. In the end, it is *your* experience, and there are a number of meaningful ways to encounter, record, and remember it. Documenting the Circuit through photos, videos, and b/vlogs can help you process the experience, remember details, and reinforce what you learned; they also let you to share the Circuit with others. It may be helpful, however, to set personal ground rules ahead of time, such as limiting the number of photos you take at a site, to safeguard the richness of the direct encounter. That said, the Jerusalem Circuit is a repeatable exercise, and one can do it differently each time—focusing on prayer, documenting the stations in detail, engaging the broader context of Jerusalem, or simply enjoying the walk.

Journals and Writing

Despite the power of visual images, we must still use language to make meaning of experience. How we experience the Circuit and the meaning we give it is ultimately determined by the words that we use, and the best way to process the Circuit is through journaling at the sites or soon after the walk is over. Effective reflection involves both thinking and writing, as connections, insights, and meanings are most fully realized when thoughts are captured—and released—through words.

Blessings and Souvenirs

For medieval pilgrims, the experience and memories of the Holy Land were supplemented by the acquisition of physical objects, or holy souvenirs, that were simply called "blessings" by both Greek (*eulogiae*) and Latin (*benedictiones*) pilgrims. Pilgrims desired a piece of Jerusalem they could take home in their pockets, such as chipped away stones, strings that measured what Jesus had touched, and ampullas full of sacred oil. Such blessings were thought to be effective against a variety of ailments. While their amulet-like properties are understood differently today, pilgrims continue the tradition of taking away material objects and physical marks of the Holy Land, from Jordan River water to Jerusalem tattoos, precisely because material reminders of spiritual encounters have significant personal meaning.

Walking the Jerusalem Circuit

Walking the Jerusalem Circuit should be likewise remembered. As well as photos, videos, writings, and sketches, items worn or carried on the walk, such as cross necklaces and prayer objects, become special mementos. Blessings can also be made along the way: from lighting candles to reviving the tradition of measuring sites with strings. While a simple souvenir can be bought along the route as a reminder of the day, mementos can also be acquired after the Circuit is over, like an icon of one of the stations.

3.

The Stations

THE SITES AND COMMEMORATIONS included below are mostly sourced from the four principal texts, but attention is given to the overall corpus of pre-Crusader writings. As previously discussed, while the primary sites are easy to identify, a full list of stations was never fixed, at least based on the texts, and there is a degree of subjectivity in selecting the material. While certain stations, like Mary the Egyptian and the Jephonias monument, may appear to be relatively minor, they were a part of Christian memory and the pilgrim experience at the time. The Western Wall Plaza may seem to be a dissonant location to remember the former Church of Holy Wisdom, but it is more or less the location, while reflecting on changes in the Jerusalem landscape over the centuries is an important aspect of the modern Circuit even if it can't be fully addressed in the book. It is also worth reflecting on the act of remembering sites that no longer exist.

We have refrained from including stations that don't clearly emerge in the texts or aren't directly on the route; similarly, we have not redressed perceived gaps in the sites and stories of Christian Jerusalem. A good example is Jesus' trial at Caiaphas's house, which includes Peter's denial of Jesus. While the commemoration was located on Mount Sion, it isn't distinctive enough in the pilgrim texts to warrant a station, although one could easily be added.[1] In short, the book seeks to depict the Jerusalem Circuit on its

---

1. The actual location of Caiaphas's house has never been identified. The Byzantine site is understood to be the present-day Armenian monastery of St. Savior directly opposite Sion Gate. St. Peter in Gallicantu, presented today as Caiaphas's house, may have previously commemorated where Peter wept after denying Christ; see Epiphanius, *Holy City* 9.

own terms (a route that, nonetheless, connected most of the principal sites in the city) rather than using the route as a means of presenting a comprehensive encounter with New Testament Jerusalem, though the distinction is not overly significant.

More arbitrary is how the book designates and numbers the stations. The initial segment of the Circuit was distinguished by the one-two movement from the Holy Sepulchre to Holy Sion. However, given the number of commemorative points in the Holy Sepulchre, as well as how the traditions of Holy Sion are now contained in separate buildings, the respective material has been separated into multiple stations. This does not necessarily represent the pilgrim experience as spaces and memories often overlapped; yet, it's the easiest way to present the material and hopefully to engage it on the ground. As a result, the Holy Sepulchre consists of five stations (stations 1–5), while Holy Sion (stations 6–7) and St. Anne's (stations 9–10) each have two. Still, some stations have multiple memories. As well as the crucifixion of Jesus, Golgotha (station 2) retains the layered memories of the tomb of Adam and Abraham's sacrifice of Isaac, while according to Christian tradition, the Last Supper and Pentecost occurred in the same room (station 6). Altogether, there are sixteen stations covering ten sites with multiple stations at the Holy Sepulchre, Holy Sion, and St. Anne's.

Entering Jerusalem

Fig. 5. Jerusalem, 785. Mosaic from the Church of St. Stephen, Umm ar-Rasas, Jordan. Photo by Dick Osseman. Used with permission.

Before setting off on the Circuit, some thought should be given to framing the experience as a pilgrimage, which can be as simple as adorning a symbol, like the Jerusalem Cross, placing a prayer object in your pocket, or saying a prayer to bless your journey. It could also include marking your departure from where you start, such as ritually crossing a threshold as you leave your building.

Unless you have lodgings in the Old City, walking the Circuit will involve entering the city on your way to the Holy Sepulchre. Pilgrimage texts indicate that pilgrims approached Jerusalem from different directions and entered through various gates. We recommend, if possible, a northern approach, which is depicted in three texts and the Madaba Map. The first text follows the entourage of Jerome (d. 420), Paula (d. 404), and her daughter, Eustochium (d. 420), who were part of an ascetic community in Bethlehem. Writing Eustochium soon after the death of her mother, Jerome recounts Paula's initial entry into Jerusalem when they arrived together in 385: Paula "passed on her left the Tomb of Helena, Queen of Abiabene . . . and entered Jerusalem." Queen Helena's tomb is the misnamed Tomb of the Kings approximately eight hundred meters north of the Damascus Gate at the juncture of Salah ed-Din Street and Nablus Road directly east of St. George's Cathedral. The text indicates that they were approaching Jerusalem from the north, taking the ancient pathway that is now Nablus Road. Keeping Helena's tomb on the left, one can walk with Paula, Eustochium, and Jerome along Nablus Road to the Damascus Gate and on to the Holy Sepulchre.

The second text is the *Life of Peter the Iberian* (c. 500), named after a fifth-century theologian and prince from Georgia. According to his *Life*, Peter visited the Martyrium of St. Stephen before entering Jerusalem on his way to the Holy Sepulchre. The martyrium is now the Basilica of St. Stephen, part of the French Dominican École Biblique, also located on Nablus Road, 350 meters north of Damascus Gate. Along with Paula, Eustochium, and Jerome, one can walk with Peter down Nablus Road through the Damascus Gate en route to the Holy Sepulchre.

The third reference is contained in the *Letter to Faustus* (c. 430), written by Eucherius, bishop of Lyons (d. c. 499): "People coming into the city from the north are taken to their first holy place by the layout of the streets, and visit the Martyrium, lately built with great magnificence by

Constantine." Once again, we can follow the text through the Damascus Gate to the Holy Sepulchre.[2]

Moving from text to visual image, the Madaba Map delineates the route from the Damascus Gate to the Holy Sepulchre. The mosaic depicts the northern gate as the city's most prominent entry point: inside the gate is a semicircular plaza with a large column and access to two cardos, which was unique for a Roman-Byzantine city.[3] The western cardo, the principal artery of the city, runs south to the eastern entrance of the Holy Sepulchre.

All of these features—the gate, the plaza, the column, and the cardos—presumably stem from Hadrian's re-founding of Jerusalem in the 130s as a Roman city renamed Aelia Capitolina (Aelia was a family name of Hadrian; Capitolina refers to the cult of Jupiter on the Capitoline Hill in Rome). In the Byzantine period, the northern approach offered Christian pilgrims a monumental pathway from the city's principal gate to the Holy Sepulchre in the middle of the city, a route that can still be traced today (present-day Khan ez-Zeit Street). Entering Jerusalem by the Damascus Gate not only allows one to walk more of the Madaba Map, you'll be accompanied on your way to the Holy Sepulchre by throngs of past pilgrims, including Paula, Eustochium, Jerome, and Peter the Iberian.

PILGRIMAGE TEXTS: ENTERING JERUSALEM

Jerome, *Letter* 108.9.1 (407): [Paula] passed on her left the Tomb of Helena, Queen of Abiabene, who brought the people corn in time of famine, and entered Jerusalem.

Eucherius, *Letter to Faustus* 5 (c. 430): People coming into the city from the north are taken to their first holy place by the layout of the streets, and visit the Martyrium, lately built with great magnificence by Constantine.

Life of Peter the Iberian, r99 (c. 500): First he went to the martyrium of St. Stephen, which was the first place he reached, and going down into the

---

2. Jerome, *Letter* 108.9.1; John Rufus, *Life of Peter the Iberian* r99; Eucherius, *Letter to Faustus* 5. For a study of the Eucherius text, see Aist, *From Topography to Text*.

3. Despite previous identifications, there are no known Christian commemorations associated with the North Gate column. See Aist, "Monument of the Miraculous Healing."

cave, he venerated his reliquary. Leaving there he hurried to holy Golgotha and the holy Tomb.

SCRIPTURE READINGS: ENTERING JERUSALEM

Psalm 48:12–14: Walk about Zion, go all around it, count its towers, consider well its ramparts; go through its citadels, that you may tell the next generation that this is God, our God forever and ever. He will be our guide forever.

Psalm 122:6–9: Pray for the peace of Jerusalem: "May they prosper who love you. Peace be within your walls, and security within your towers." For the sake of my relatives and friends I will say, "Peace be within you." For the sake of the house of the Lord our God, I will seek your good.

Stations 1–5
The Holy Sepulchre

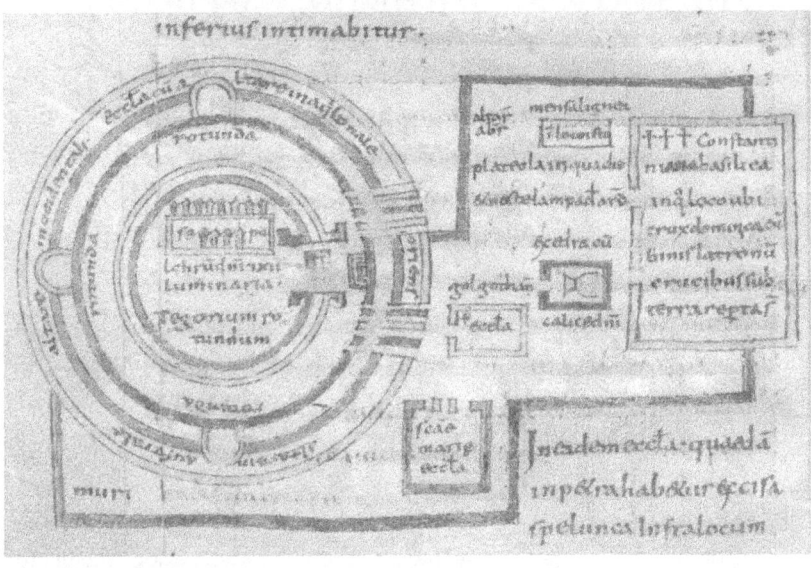

Fig. 6. The Church of the Holy Sepulchre. Vienna, Österreichische Nationalbibliothek, Cod. 458, fol. 4v. Used with permission. Ninth-century manuscript drawing based on the late seventh-century prototype in Adomnán, *De locis sanctis*.

THE COMPLEX OF THE HOLY SEPULCHRE

For medieval pilgrims, the Holy Sepulchre had three principal commemorations: Jesus' resurrection (the tomb of Christ), Jesus' crucifixion (Golgotha), and the place where the Holy Cross was found (the Basilica of Constantine). Complementing this threefold focus were supplemental memories and sacred objects, such as the tomb of Adam, Abraham's sacrifice of Isaac, the crucifixion relics of the lance and the sponge, the rock that sealed Christ's tomb, the miraculous healing of the Holy Cross, the center of the world, and the conversion of Mary the Egyptian. As the central site of Christendom, the Holy Sepulchre was a repository of Christian holiness, and we can speak in terms of its "commemorative fabric." The complex was not merely an assemblage of sites and relics; rather, the entire grounds of the Holy Sepulchre, both its indoor and outdoor spaces, were seen by pilgrims as a unified whole that set it apart from the rest of Jerusalem's commemorative landscape.

THE STATIONS OF THE HOLY SEPULCHRE

The Holy Sepulchre material is divided into five stations:

- **Station 1: The Tomb of Christ.** Also known as the aedicule ("the little house"), the tomb commemorated the burial and resurrection of Jesus.
- **Station 2: Golgotha.** The rock of Golgotha (Hebrew), or Calvary (Latin), commemorated the crucifixion of Jesus, as well as Abraham's sacrifice of Isaac and the tomb of Adam.
- **Station 3: The Holy Cross.** During the pre-Crusader period, the place where the Holy Cross was found was in the central apse of the Basilica of Constantine, destroyed in 1009. Since the Crusader period, it has been associated with the lower crypt, now the Franciscan Chapel of the Finding of the Cross.
- **Station 4: The Center of the World.** Located in various places throughout the complex during the pre-Crusader period, the center of the world is commemorated today in the Katholicon, the primary Greek Orthodox liturgical space, opposite the tomb of Christ.
- **Station 5: The Conversion of Mary the Egyptian.** The event occurred at the eastern façade of the Basilica of Constantine. After the destruction of the church, the memory moved to the southern courtyard (parvis), where a chapel is dedicated to her.

The Stations

THE PRE-CRUSADER SITE

Formerly a Jewish cemetery, the grounds of the Holy Sepulchre were outside the city walls at the time of Jesus' execution. The area was quarried as early as the eighth century BCE and was eventually abandoned: its exposed surfaces provided an ideal setting for rock-cut tombs. Known as Golgotha (the place of the skull), the former quarry was also used for Roman crucifixions.

Within a decade of Jesus' death, the walls of Jerusalem were expanded to the north by King Agrippa I (d. 44), incorporating Golgotha into the city, though the site presumably remained undeveloped, open to the elements, and accessible to the public. It is likewise presumed that Christians visited the site, venerating the tomb, perhaps marking it with symbols and inscriptions; indeed, the following argument requires that Christians knew where the tomb was and that others, namely, the Romans, knew that the Christians knew.

Around 130, Emperor Hadrian (d. 138) refounded Jerusalem as a Roman city, taking the name Aelia Capitolina. His urban project included a Roman temple dedicated to Aphrodite (Venus) built over and burying the tomb of Christ. This is certainly what fourth-century Christians believed: that Hadrian placed the Roman temple on the Christian site to erase its memory. According to Eusebius (d. 339),

> Godless people . . . had covered up this divine memorial of immortality in order that it should be forgotten. With much labor, they brought in soil from elsewhere and covered the whole site, and by raising the level and laying a stone pavement, they concealed the divine cave under a heap of earth. And, as though this were not enough, they built above ground . . . a gloomy shrine of lifeless idols dedicated to the impure demon Aphrodite, where they poured foul libations on profane and accursed altars.[4]

Just as Christian knowledge of the tomb's location prior to the Roman temple is necessary, the authenticity of the site depends upon Christians retaining memory of the buried tomb for two centuries: between the construction of the temple in the 130s and the excavation of the site in the 320s when it was rediscovered.

After assuming power in the East in 324, Constantine called the Council of Nicaea in 325. Macarius, the bishop of Jerusalem, attended the council, and the two discussed plans for developing Christian Jerusalem

---

4. Eusebius, *Life of Constantine* 3.26.

focusing on the tomb of Christ. Based on local knowledge that the tomb was beneath the Roman temple, Constantine ordered the excavation of the site. Eusebius, a contemporary eyewitness, depicts the rediscovery of the tomb as nothing less than its own resurrection: "The venerable and most holy testimony of the Saviour's resurrection, beyond all our hopes, came into view; the holy of holies, the Cave, was, like our Saviour, 'restored to life' . . . by its very existence bearing clearer testimony to the resurrection of the Saviour than any words."[5]

Barring no expense, Constantine—who "realized that he ought to render the most blessed place of the Saviour's Resurrection in Jerusalem attractive and worthy of veneration by all"—sent detailed instructions to Macarius for a "house of prayer" to be erected, a complex that would stretch from the tomb eastward to the city's western cardo.[6] The rock mass surrounding the tomb was leveled within a radius of twenty meters until all that remained was a rock shell that preserved the interior space of the burial chamber. The tomb's exterior was covered in marble and embellished with gold and silver forming a little house, or aedicule.

We have yet to mention Constantine's mother, Helena, in connection with the project. Tradition attributes to Helena the building of the Holy Sepulchre as well as the finding of the Holy Cross. This is based on her visit to Jerusalem, which has been generally dated to 326, the year following the Council of Nicaea. Recent scholarship has redated her sojourn to 328—well after work on the Holy Sepulchre had begun.[7] Helena was involved in the development of the Holy Land and played an important role in linking local traditions with imperial possibilities: Eusebius credits her with founding the slightly later churches at Bethlehem and the Mount of Olives; he's silent, however, on Helena's contributions to the Holy Sepulchre.

The revised date of Helena's visit not only means that the construction of the Holy Sepulchre was already in progress when she arrived, it excludes the possibility that she discovered the True Cross during the excavation of the Roman temple. That doesn't mean that she didn't have any involvement with the relics: she was possibly presented with some previously identified

---

5. Eusebius, *Life of Constantine* 3.28.
6. Eusebius, *Life of Constantine* 3.25.
7. See Hillner, *Helena Augusta*, 204–44. Based upon correspondence between Constantine and Macarius following the Council of Nicaea, the date of the excavation of the Roman temple and commencement on the Holy Sepulchre remains the same: 326.

The Stations

objects, and while a sizable piece of the True Cross remained in Jerusalem, she may have taken some wood and nails back with her to Italy.[8]

Along with omitting Helena, Eusebius focuses solely on the tomb; he never mentions Golgotha, the Cross, or the place of the crucifixion. Early Christian sources often downplayed Jesus' execution as a criminal, but Eusebius's silence means that we have no contemporary information on the crucifixion site.

Built between 326 and 335, the Holy Sepulchre was dedicated on September 13, 335 (work on the Anastasis continued for a number of years). From west to east, the main features of the complex, comprising a total area of approximately 130 x 60 meters (426 x 196 feet), were: (1) a round building approximately thirty-seven meters (120 feet) in diameter, called the Anastasis, or Rotunda, that housed the tomb of Christ, (2) an inner courtyard, and (3) a large double-aisled basilica, known as the Martyrium, or the Basilica of Constantine, which was oriented to the west in the direction of the tomb. The Rotunda was crowned with a wooden cupola with a circular opening in the center.[9] The place of the crucifixion was on top of a rocky outcrop of poor unquarried rock that could be approached from the western end of the basilica's southern aisles; it could also be seen in the southeastern corner of the inner courtyard. East of the basilica, an outer courtyard and a monumental entrance connected the Holy Sepulchre to the cardo. Reversing directions, pilgrims entered the complex from the east, encountering Golgotha before reaching the tomb.

Damage inflicted by the Persians in 614 was not severe, and the complex was repaired by the patriarch Modestus: subsequent pilgrim descriptions have a similar amount of commemorative details and religious imagination as Byzantine texts. In 638, when Sophronius, the Christian patriarch of Jerusalem, was showing the caliph 'Umar around the Holy Sepulchre as part of the handover of the city, 'Umar refused to pray at the appointed time of Muslim prayer stating that if he did so his followers would turn the church into a mosque.[10] The act forms the basis of the so-called Pact of 'Umar, which offers a constructive talking point for interfaith relations today.

---

8. See Ambrose, *On the Death of Theodosius*, which is the earliest extant source that connects Helena to the Holy Cross. Ambrose states that Helena brought two of the nails back to Italy (she threw one in the sea to quiet a storm). Today, the cathedrals of Milan and Monza each possess a relic allegedly containing one of the nails. Also see Drijvers, *Helena Augusta*.

9. Magness, *Jerusalem*, 356.

10. A portico in the outer atrium was later used for Muslim prayer.

Despite earthquakes, fires, conquests, and riots, the Constantinian complex remained essentially intact until its destruction in 1009, enacted upon the orders of the Fatimid caliph al-Hakim (d. 1021). The Byzantine emperor Constantine Monomachos (d. 1055) made a modest restoration of the complex in 1048 prior to the arrival of the Crusader armies in 1099. Today, the Holy Sepulchre is essentially the building that the Crusaders dedicated on July 15, 1149—a twelfth-century restoration of a fourth-century complex substantially destroyed in 1009. Among the major changes, the primary entrance was moved to the south; the inner courtyard was domed, and the basilica was never rebuilt: the basilica grounds were turned into a cloister for Augustinian canons, while the area underneath was opened up as a crypt. The Rotunda was capped with a conical roof with an oculus; the dome was last restored in 1979–80. To understand the contemporary site, familiarize yourself with its original Constantinian layout (see fig. 7).[11]

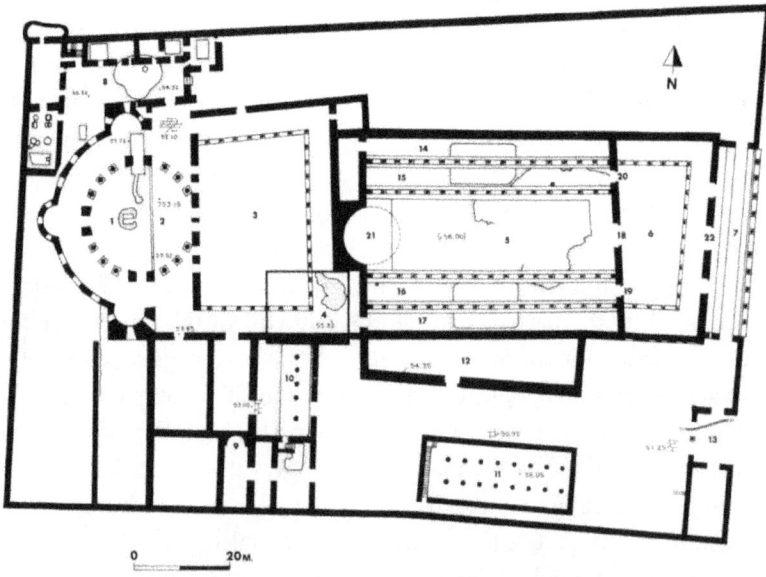

Fig. 7. The Church of the Holy Sepulchre, the Byzantine church complex. From Gibson and Taylor, *Beneath the Church*, 75, fig. 45. With permission of Shimon Gibson.

---

11. Due to subsequent archaeological findings, Gibson has since retracted the northern wall of the complex.

The Stations

THE ORDER OF THE SITES

The tomb of Christ was the destination of Holy Land pilgrimage. Consequently, the majority of pilgrimage texts commence their account of Jerusalem with the Holy Sepulchre, which is described in one of two ways: either east-to-west, ending with the tomb, or west-to-east, beginning with the tomb. In either direction, relics and secondary commemorations are generally mentioned along the way.

- **East-to-West.** Following the architectural layout of the complex from its entrance off the western cardo, pilgrims proceeded in a westerly direction, passing the place of the Holy Cross (the Basilica of Constantine) before coming to Golgotha and concluding with the tomb of Christ. Therefore, on their way in, pilgrims encountered Jesus' crucifixion and resurrection in narrative order.
- **West-to-East.** Other texts start with the tomb, the focal point of the complex, moving in an easterly direction to Golgotha and the place of the Holy Cross (the basilica) before coming to the western cardo.

From the Holy Sepulchre, the texts commonly proceed through the intramural city to sites beyond the walls. Thus, Jerusalem is described from the inside out.

Today, one enters the Holy Sepulchre from the south, walking immediately into the middle of the passion story: Golgotha is on the right; the tomb is over to the left, and the stone of anointing is straight ahead. Notwithstanding the primacy of the resurrection, there is not a determinative order for visiting the Holy Sepulchre or marking stations 1–5. We will begin with the tomb of Christ, followed by Golgotha and the Holy Cross, before discussing the center of the world and the conversion of Mary the Egyptian.

Fig. 8. *The Church of the Holy Sepulchre, Jerusalem*, c. 1546. Domenico dalle Greche (Italian, active 1543–58). Woodcut. The Metropolitan Museum of Art. Open Access. Public domain.

Station 1
The Tomb of Christ

THE STATION

The tomb of Christ in the center of the Anastasis.

Fig. 9. Ampulla 9. Palestinian workshop. Reliquary ampulla containing oil from holy places, alloy of lead and tin, silver, late sixth–early seventh century. Monza, Museum and Treasury of Monza Cathedral. © Museo e Tesoro del Duomo di Monza/photo Piero Pozzi. Used with permission.

COMMEMORATING STATION 1: THE TOMB OF CHRIST

Commence the Jerusalem Circuit with a visit inside the tomb of Christ; however, queues are often long, with even minimum waits often thirty to forty-five minutes. Since the Circuit will take around four to six hours to complete, not including navigating the opening hours of later sites, you may not have time to enter the tomb. The important thing is to *commemorate* the station, which can be done by walking around the aedicule, reflecting upon the burial and resurrection of Jesus, and thinking about the tomb as a focus of Christian piety for two millenniums.

- Begin in prayer.
- Review the information on the Holy Sepulchre (above).
- Read the background information, pilgrimage texts, and Scripture readings for the tomb of Christ.
- If possible, read Eusebius, *Life of Constantine* 3.25–40.[12]
- Make a full circuit around the aedicule.
- Reflect upon the burial and resurrection of Jesus. What details emerge from the story? How does being present in the setting inform and/or obscure the story?
- Observe other pilgrims and religious persons around the aedicule. Speak to a few. What countries and traditions are they from?
- Observe the front of the aedicule in detail. Identify the symbols of the Greeks, Franciscans, and Armenians on the candlesticks and lamps.
- Reflect on the role of angels in the resurrection story. Look for angels on the façade of the aedicule and inside the tomb. Also, the anteroom of the aedicule is called the Chapel of the Angel.
- Find the so-called tomb of Joseph of Arimathea that dates to the time of Jesus (the late Second Temple period). It is accessed from a recess behind the tomb of Christ: facing away from the aedicule, the entrance is slightly to the right.
- Light a candle, if you wish.
- End in prayer.

---

12. The text can be found at: https://www.newadvent.org/fathers/25023.htm.

The Stations

BACKGROUND INFORMATION: THE TOMB OF CHRIST

The first-century site was an east-facing tomb carved into a west-rising mass of rock in the midst of an abandoned quarry. Inside the tomb on the right (to the north) was a burial bench cut into the wall, a style known as an arcosolium tomb. The location of the burial bench corresponds with the reference in Mark 16:5 to the young man dressed in white sitting on the right side of the tomb as the women entered.

While it is possible that the tomb had more than one burial shelf, the focus on it being newly cut implies that Jesus' body was the only one inside the tomb. As circumstantial evidence of the resurrection, this is an important detail—Jesus was the only one buried there, and by the third day, the tomb didn't contain *any* bodies.

To review material previously discussed, after Golgotha was incorporated into the city, the tomb remained accessible to the Christian community, who may have marked it with decorations and inscriptions that were later used to identify the tomb in the fourth century. In the 130s, Emperor Hadrian covered the site with a Roman temple dedicated to Aphrodite (Venus). The argument demands that for two hundred years the Christian community remembered the temple as the place of Jesus' resurrection. The contemporary report of Eusebius records the recovery of the tomb in the 320s: orders were given by Constantine to excavate the Roman temple, and layer upon layer of its foundation was removed until the tomb was discovered.

The words of Eusebius are worth repeating: Emperor Constantine "realized that he ought to render the most blessed place of the Saviour's Resurrection in Jerusalem attractive and worthy of veneration by all." However, "godless people . . . had covered up this divine memorial of immortality in order that it should be forgotten." Constantine ordered the removal of the Roman temple, and work was carried out until "the venerable and most holy testimony of the Saviour's resurrection, beyond all our hopes, came into view; the holy of holies, the Cave, was, like our Savior, 'restored to life' . . . by its very existence bearing clearer testimony to the resurrection of the Saviour than any words."[13]

The rock around the tomb was cut away until only a shell of living rock remained, which retained the integrity of the empty space inside. The

---

13. Eusebius, *Life of Constantine* 3.25–28.

floor was leveled around the tomb for nearly twenty meters in every direction. The tomb's exterior rock was clad with marble, decorated with gold and silver, and crowned by a cross. After nearly ten years of construction, the Holy Sepulchre was dedicated on September 13, 325.

We have a good sense of what the aedicule looked like: our evidence comes from pilgrim ampullas embossed with images of the resurrection. The ampullas show how Christian imagination blended biblical memory with contemporary features. While the images contain angels and the women at the tomb, Jesus' grave is not depicted in its original form as one might envision from the Gospel accounts; instead, the *aedicule* has been placed in the middle of the biblical scene! The most impressive collections of Byzantine ampullas from Jerusalem are in museums in Monza and Bobbio, Italy (see fig. 9).[14]

The use of ampullas is implied by the Piacenza Pilgrim, who visited Christ's tomb around the year 570: "A bronze lamp burns day and night at the place where his head was; we took a blessing from the lamp [filling an ampulla with oil], and put it back in its place." The comment also reveals how past tradition continues in the present: today, upon entering the tomb chamber (and turning to the right), a canister of candles is on the left (west) side of the burial bench. Following Jewish tradition, Jesus' body would have been placed on the bench with his head to the west, thus, facing the rising sun to the east. In short, the canister of lit candles is in the same place where the Piacenza Pilgrim noted the bronze lamp over 1,400 years ago: a flame at the head of Christ commemorating the resurrected light of the world!

Due to destruction, fire, and general restorations, there have been at least four iterations of the aedicule—335, post-1009, 1555, and 1810—rebuilt around what remains of the natural stone of the tomb.[15] The current aedicule dates from 1810 following the fire of 1808, an opportunity the Greeks used to solidify their standing as the dominant presence in the Holy Sepulchre.

One notable change has occurred in the aedicule over the years: what was originally an open porch with supporting columns has since been enclosed, creating an anteroom known today as the Chapel of the Angel that

---

14. According to tradition, the ampullas were given to the Lombard queen Theodelina (d. 628); the materials and high quality of the workmanship suggests that they were intended as royal gifts. Ordinary pilgrims would have used ceramic ampullas. See Magness, *Jerusalem*, 380–84.

15. For a study of the history of the aedicule, see Biddle, *Tomb of Christ*. The burial chamber of the aedicule was briefly dismantled in 2016, exposing some of the original limestone. See Romney, "Jesus' Tomb."

one enters prior to the burial chamber. A waist-high pedestal in the middle of the chapel contains a stone cube that purportedly derives from the stone that sealed the tomb. An important witness of the resurrection, a relic of the stone is consistently noted in the pilgrim texts.

The dome of the Anastasis, most recently restored in 1979–80, is the larger of the two domes covering the Holy Sepulchre. Its interior decorations, dedicated in 1997, consist of twelve rays representing the apostles taking the good news from the center of the world to the ends of the earth; each ray is tipped with three points symbolizing the Trinity. The design is set against a mother-of-pearl background that symbolizes the luminous cloud that led the Israelites into the desert.[16]

PILGRIMAGE TEXTS: THE TOMB OF CHRIST

Jerome, *Letter* **108.9.2 (385):** On entering the Tomb of the Resurrection, [Paula] kissed the stone which the angel removed from the sepulchre door; then like a thirsty man who has waited long, and at last comes to water, she faithfully kissed the very shelf on which the Lord's body had lain. Her tears and lamentations there are known to all Jerusalem—or rather to the Lord himself to whom she was praying.

The Piacenza Pilgrim, *Travels* **18 (c. 570):** Kneeling down and kissing the ground, we entered into the Holy City, in which we venerated the Lord's tomb. The tomb has been cut out of living rock, or rather cut out of the rock itself, where the body of the Lord Jesus Christ was placed. A bronze lamp burns day and night at the place where his head was; we took a blessing from the lamp and put it back in its place. Earth from outside is brought into the tomb, and those who enter take some away as a blessing. The very stone, with which the tomb was closed, is in front of the mouth of the tomb and is the same color of rock, as it was cut from the rock of Golgotha. Now this stone is decorated with gold and precious stones, but the rock of the tomb is like a millstone. There are a countless ornaments hanging from iron rods: armlets, bracelets, necklaces, rings, headbands, plaited girdles, belts, crowns of emperors with gold and precious stones and adornments of an empress. The tomb is covered with a cone of silver with golden rays. An altar has been placed in front of the tomb.

16. On the process and controversies of completing the design, see Cohen, *Saving the Holy Sepulchre*, 226–35.

Adomnán (Arculf), *On the Holy Places* 1.3 (680s): Arculf reports that [the stone that was rolled against the door of the tomb] was split, and divided into two pieces. The smaller piece has been shaped and squared up into an altar, which is to be seen set up . . . in front of the door of the Lord's Tomb. . . . The larger part of this stone has also been cut to shape, and forms a second square altar which stands, covered with linen, in a position at the east of this church.

Hugeburc (Willibald), *Life of Willibald* 18 (724-26): And near there is the garden in which was the Saviour's tomb. The tomb had been carved out of rock, and the rock stands up out of the ground: at the bottom it is square, but it is pointed on top. The tomb is now surmounted by a cross, and there is now a remarkable building over it. On the east of the tomb, in the actual rock, a door has been made, through which people enter the tomb for prayer. And inside there is a shelf on which the Lord's body lay. Fifteen golden bowls stand on the shelf. They are filled with oil, and burn day and night. The shelf on which the Lord's body lay is inside the rock of the tomb on the north side, that is, on the right side as one enters the tomb to prayer. And there also, in front of the tomb door, lies a large square stone, like the original stone which the angel rolled away from the tomb door.

SCRIPTURE READINGS: THE TOMB OF CHRIST

Luke 23:50-56 (The burial of Jesus): Now there was a good and righteous man named Joseph, who, though a member of the council, had not agreed to their plan and action. He came from the Jewish town of Arimathea, and he was waiting expectantly for the kingdom of God. This man went to Pilate and asked for the body of Jesus. Then he took it down, wrapped it in a linen cloth, and laid it in a rock-hewn tomb where no one had ever been laid. It was the day of Preparation, and the sabbath was beginning. The women who had come with him from Galilee followed, and they saw the tomb and how his body was laid. Then they returned, and prepared spices and ointments. On the sabbath they rested according to the commandment.

John 19:38-42 (The burial of Jesus): After these things, Joseph of Arimathea, who was a disciple of Jesus, though a secret one because of his fear of the Jews, asked Pilate to let him take away the body of Jesus. Pilate gave him permission; so he came and removed his body. Nicodemus, who had at first come to Jesus by night, also came, bringing a mixture of myrrh and aloes, weighing about a hundred pounds. They took the body of Jesus and wrapped it with the spices in linen cloths, according to the burial custom of the Jews. Now there was a garden in the place where he was crucified, and in the garden there was a new tomb in which no one had ever been laid. And so, because it was the Jewish day of Preparation, and the tomb was nearby, they laid Jesus there.

Luke 24:1–12 (The resurrection of Jesus): But on the first day of the week, at early dawn, they came to the tomb, taking the spices that they had prepared. They found the stone rolled away from the tomb, but when they went in, they did not find the body. While they were perplexed about this, suddenly two men in dazzling clothes stood beside them. The women were terrified and bowed their faces to the ground, but the men said to them, "Why do you look for the living among the dead? He is not here, but has risen. Remember how he told you, while he was still in Galilee, that the Son of Man must be handed over to sinners, and be crucified, and on the third day rise again." Then they remembered his words, and returning from the tomb, they told all this to the eleven and to all the rest. Now it was Mary Magdalene, Joanna, Mary the mother of James, and the other women with them who told this to the apostles. But these words seemed to them an idle tale, and they did not believe them. But Peter got up and ran to the tomb; stooping and looking in, he saw the linen cloths by themselves; then he went home, amazed at what had happened.

John 20:1–18 (The resurrection of Jesus): Early on the first day of the week, while it was still dark, Mary Magdalene came to the tomb and saw that the stone had been removed from the tomb. So she ran and went to Simon Peter and the other disciple, the one whom Jesus loved, and said to them, "They have taken the Lord out of the tomb, and we do not know where they have laid him." Then Peter and the other disciple set out and went towards the tomb. The two were running together, but the other disciple outran Peter and reached the tomb first. He bent down to look in and saw the linen wrappings lying there, but he did not go in. Then Simon Peter came, following him, and went into the tomb. He saw the linen wrappings lying there, and the cloth that had been on Jesus' head, not lying with the linen wrappings but rolled up in a place by itself. Then the other disciple, who reached the tomb first, also went in, and he saw and believed; for as yet they did not understand the scripture, that he must rise from the dead. Then the disciples returned to their homes.

But Mary stood weeping outside the tomb. As she wept, she bent over to look into the tomb; and she saw two angels in white, sitting where the body of Jesus had been lying, one at the head and the other at the feet. They said to her, "Woman, why are you weeping?" She said to them, "They have taken away my Lord, and I do not know where they have laid him." When she had said this, she turned around and saw Jesus standing there, but she did not know that it was Jesus. Jesus said to her, "Woman, why are you weeping? Whom are you looking for?" Supposing him to be the gardener, she said to him, "Sir, if you have carried him away, tell me where you have laid him, and I will take him away." Jesus said to her, "Mary!" She turned and said to him in Hebrew, "Rabbouni!" (which means Teacher). Jesus said to her, "Do not hold on to me, because I have not yet ascended to the Father. But go to my brothers and say to them, 'I am ascending to my Father and your Father, to my God and your God.'" Mary Magdalene went and announced to the disciples, "I have seen the Lord"; and she told them that he had said these things to her.

Station 2
Golgotha

THE STATION

Golgotha (Hebrew), also known as Calvary (Latin), is immediately on the right as you enter the Holy Sepulchre. The upper chapels commemorate Jesus' crucifixion. The unadorned chapel at ground level is the tomb of Adam. The station is consequently divided into two parts.

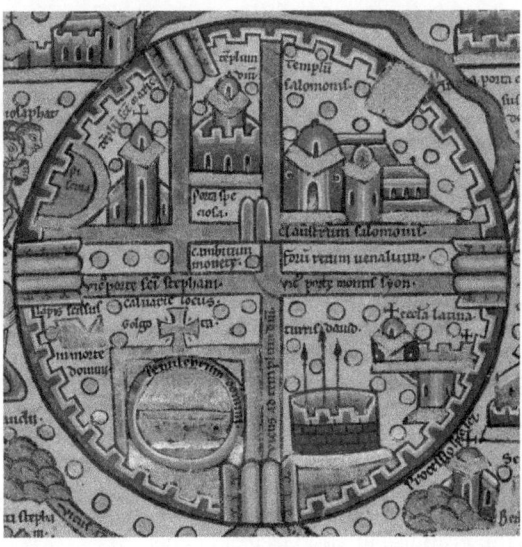

Fig. 10. The Hague Map of Jerusalem, c. 1170. Golgotha and the Sepulchre of the Lord in the lower left quadrant. The Hague, Koninklijke Bibliotheek, 76 F 5, fol. 1r sc. 1. Public domain.

COMMEMORATING STATION 2: GOLGOTHA

Begin with the upper chapels of Golgotha, which are reached by nineteen steps immediately inside the front entrance of the building. The upper level is subdivided into two adjacent chapels: a Franciscan chapel on the right and a Greek chapel on the left, which faces the rock of Golgotha. The place of the crucifixion is marked by a round metal plate with an aperture in the middle located underneath the altar table in the Greek chapel: think of the plate as a "commemorative socket" supporting the cross. The aperture allows pilgrims to touch the rock below.

Pilgrims engage the place of the crucifixion in various ways. Some kneel under the altar, touch the rock, and kiss the plate. Others stand at a distance. Immerse yourself in the setting, mindful that remembering the death of Jesus can evoke an emotional reaction in pilgrims. Although one can generally move about the chapels, especially in the back, the area can be crowded at times. There is often a queue for the place of the cross, though waiting in line allows time to observe the setting as well as other pilgrims. There are places to sit in silence. After spending time in the upper chapels, descend the opposite staircase to the tomb of Adam.

- Begin in prayer.
- Read the background information, pilgrimage texts, and Scripture readings for Golgotha.
- Spend time in the first bay of the Franciscan chapel, which is dedicated to the Old Testament.
- Observe the wall mosaic on the right, *The Sacrifice of Isaac*. How does the sacrifice of Isaac prefigure the crucifixion event in Christian thought (i.e., a father sacrificing a son)? How are the two events similar and dissimilar?
- Proceed to the second bay. Observe the details of the wall mosaics, *St. John and the Holy Women* (on the right) and *Jesus Is Nailed to the Cross* (straight ahead). Locate the Crusader mosaic of *Christ in Ascension* above your head.
- Note the altar to Our Lady of Sorrows (*Stabat Mater*) at the threshold between the Franciscan and Greek chapels.
- Continue into the Greek area. Observe the visible sections of the rock of Calvary.

- Stand before or kneel under the altar table. The aperture in the round plate marks the traditional place of the crucifixion. Touch it or kiss it. Take a photo; say a prayer.
- There is another image of the sacrifice of Isaac immediately past the crucifixion altar. Next to it are icons of Jesus' nativity. What does Christmas feel like from the perspective of Calvary?
- Light a candle at the prayer station, if you wish.
- Spend time in open-eyed prayer looking at the images, decorations, and accoutrements in the Greek chapel.
- The paintings on the walls and ceiling of the Greek chapel tell the story of Jesus' passion from Gethsemane to the Cross. They are read in sequence as one approaches the altar from the back of the chapel.
- Observe others around you.
- Descend the opposite steps to the Chapel of Adam.

BACKGROUND INFORMATION: GOLGOTHA

John 19:17 states that Jesus was crucified at Golgotha (Hebrew), which means "the place of the skull" (Calvary is the Latin equivalent). Although it has come to specify the particular place of Jesus' execution, Golgotha referred to the general grounds of the quarry. The area was used as a cemetery, but it is not clear what the reference to the skull signifies. Did the appearance of the place resemble the shape of a skull, which is often assumed, or does it refer to something else? Leaving the precision of the x-marks-the-spot aside, the general setting of Jesus' crucifixion is highly credible: the Romans utilized a disused quarry just outside the walls, itself a Jewish cemetery, as a visible location for public executions.

Scholars use the language of a rocky outcrop to describe the first-century site, while Golgotha today is also referred to as a column, a pillar, and a block of stone. The formation is a tall vertical column of living rock standing between nine and fourteen meters above the surrounding bedrock with a top surface area of approximately four square meters.[17] What remains unclear is the degree to which the rock resembles its first-century appearance, and similarly, how it looked in the fourth century prior to being enshrined

---

17. On the dimensions of the rock, see Gibson and Taylor, *Beneath the Church*, 57.

in the Holy Sepulchre. Is the rocky outcrop more or less as it was? If so, it's hard to imagine one, let alone three crucifixions, on top of the relatively high and narrow block of stone. Or was it substantially reduced at the time the Holy Sepulchre was built? The preparation of the aedicule—cutting the mass of stone away from the tomb and leveling the floor of the Anastasis—was a massive project. Something similar could have been done with Golgotha, but we don't know.

In short, our pre-Constantinian understanding of the rock of Golgotha is speculative. Though less important to early Christians than the place of the resurrection, as with the tomb, oral tradition may have associated Jesus' crucifixion with a specific location, namely, the rocky outcrop. Likewise, Christians may have marked it in some way prior to the Roman temple. The temple, in turn, presumably concealed it, but it's unclear what meaning the Romans gave to the rock, or what they thought the Christians believed. Writing years later, Jerome states that a statue to Venus was placed on the rock where the cross had stood, but we're not entirely sure.[18] In any case, after the Roman temple was excavated, the Constantinian complex incorporated the rock pillar, identified as Golgotha, as one of its primary features.

All told, we should look for the place of the crucifixion in relation to the tomb, not the other way around. Again, what we glean from Eusebius is that the discovery of the tomb took precedence over Golgotha, suggesting that the latter was established after the tomb was found. Although pilgrims today are often struck by how close the two are to each other, their proximity is affirmed by John 19:42, which states that Jesus was buried in a tomb *nearby* the place of his crucifixion. As sparse as it is, the biblical reference was presumably a factor in (re)identifying the site in the fourth century. If the rock wasn't marked or remembered in a recognizable way, then the Constantinian project was left to choose a nearby location with notable features. The scenario does little to diminish the general authenticity of the site. Uncontested in early Christian tradition, the area of the Holy Sepulchre remains the most credible location of biblical Golgotha, and Jesus was likely crucified on or near the enshrined rock, not far from the tomb.

What we can say with certainty is that the rock of Calvary is poor, unquarried stone. While the area around Golgotha was mined for its prized limestone, a column of unusable stone was left untouched. Although it is not mentioned in the pilgrim texts, the rock is rejected stone—unquarried

---

18. Jerome, *Letter* 58.3.

material unsuitable for building—a physical attribute of the crucifixion site that appeals metaphorically to biblical Christology. Identifying Ps 118:22 with Jesus, Acts 4:11 declares that the stone rejected by the builders has become the cornerstone. Regardless of how the rock was identified as Golgotha, from a *commemorative standpoint*, the place of Jesus' crucifixion is, in fact, a mass of rejected stone.

Christian thought has associated Golgotha with two Old Testament figures, Abraham and Adam. Abraham's sacrifice of Isaac prefigured God's offering of his own son, Jesus, with Golgotha identified as Mount Moriah, despite the latter's identification with the temple (see 2 Chr 3:1). Mentioned in the pilgrim texts, the Holy Sepulchre has long maintained an altar to Abraham. Today, a large mosaic of Abraham's sacrifice of Isaac adorns the Franciscan chapel, while a Greek chapel dedicated to Abraham is located immediately above Golgotha, which is part of the monastery of Abraham that extends to the south. The tomb of Adam is discussed below.

Turning to the commemorative details of the upper chapels, the Franciscan chapel moves from the Old to the New Testament, while the Greek chapel depicts scenes from Gethsemane to Golgotha. The first bay in the Franciscan area is dedicated to Old Testament prophecies and prefigurations of the crucifixion. The large wall mosaic, *The Sacrifice of Isaac*, was designed by the Italian artist Luigi Trifoglio (d. 1939) in 1925, while the ceiling vault contains portraits of four Old Testament writers by Pietro D'Achiardi (d. 1940) with accompanying verses in Latin:

- Nearest the wall: King David
  Foderunt manus meas et pedes meos.
  "They pierced my hands and my feet" (Ps 22:16).

- Nearest the stairwell: Isaiah
  Vulneratus est propter iniquitates nostras.
  "He was wounded on account of our transgressions" (Isa 53:5).

- Opposite the wall: Zechariah
  Aspicient ad me quem confixerunt.
  "They will look upon me whom they have pierced" (Zech 12:10).

- Opposite the stairwell: Daniel
  Et post hebdomades sexaginta duas occidentur Christus.
  "After the sixty-two weeks, an anointed one shall be cut off" (Dan 9:26).

On the archway nearest the stairway are words from Isa 53:4: *Vere languores nostros ipse tulit et dolores nostros ipse portavit et nos putavimus eum quasi leprosum et percussum a Deo et humiliatum* ("Surely he has borne our infirmities and carried our diseases; yet we accounted him stricken, struck down by God, and afflicted"); the archway opposite the wall carries the ensuing text from Isa 53:7: *Oblatus est quia ipse voluit, et non aperuit os suum; sicut ovis ad occisionem ducetur* ("He was oppressed, even as he willed, but he did not open his mouth; like a lamb that is led to the slaughter").[19] Supplementing the bay's theme as the journey to the cross through the Old Testament, ceiling figures include Adam, Eve, Cain, and Abel.

With the second bay of the Franciscan chapel, one enters the New Testament. Foreshadowing the victory of the crucifixion, the ceiling vault boasts a twelfth-century Crusader mosaic of *Christ in Ascension* as well as modern images of Peter and Paul. The two wall mosaics, also designed by Luigi Trifoglio in 1925, detail scenes of the passion. On the right, *St. John and the Holy Women* (John 19:25–27) invites pilgrims to join the witnesses of the crucifixion. Straight ahead, *Jesus Is Nailed to the Cross* marks the eleventh station of the Way of the Cross. Although Jesus is not yet hanging on the cross, the mosaic depicts Jesus' mother standing behind him, a feature of the medieval devotional tradition of *Stabat Mater*, based on a hymn that depicts a suffering Mary standing near the cross during Jesus' crucifixion. A subject of both art and music, *Stabat Mater* opens with the line: *Stabat mater dolorosa iuxta crucem lacrimosa, dum pendebat filius* ("The sorrowful mother was standing near the cross weeping, while her son was hanging"). The words on the arch opening to the Greek chapel allude to the hymn; the small altar with a bust of Mary is dedicated to Our Lady of Sorrows.

With views of the rock before you, proceed to the altar table in the Greek chapel. Under the table marking the place of the crucifixion, a round metal plate with a hole in the middle represents the socket that held the cross. Stand near or kneel under the table. Say a prayer; touch the rock or kiss the plate; take a photo, or simply observe the setting. There are stations for lighting candles. The ceiling and piers of the Greek chapel contain images of Jesus' passion, including Gethsemane (see fig. 20), his trial before Pilate, and the crucifixion. To read the images in sequence, start at the back of the chapel near the staircase and proceed forward.

---

19. NRSV here is amended to match the slightly different Latin version of the verse; modern English translations of the Hebrew read "he was oppressed and he was afflicted."

THE STATIONS

PILGRIMAGE TEXTS: GOLGOTHA

Jerome, *Letter* 108.9.2 (407): [Paula] fell down and worshipped before the Cross as if she could see the Lord hanging on it.

The Piacenza Pilgrim, *Travels* 19 (c. 570): From the tomb, it is eighty paces to Golgotha. You go up on one side of it by the very steps which our Lord went to be crucified. You can see the place where he was crucified, and on the actual rock there is a bloodstain. Beside this is the altar of Abraham, which is where he intended to offer Isaac, and where Melchizedek offered sacrifice. Next to the altar is a crack, and if you put your ear to it, you hear streams of water. If you throw an apple into it, or anything else that will float, and then go to Siloam, you can pick it up there.

Adomnán (Arculf), *On the Holy Places* 1.5 (680s): Further to the east has been built another huge church on the site which in Hebrew is called Golgotha. From the roof hangs a large bronze wheel for lamps, and below it stands a great silver cross, fixed in the same socket as the wooden cross on which the Saviour of mankind once suffered. There is a cave in this Church, cut into the rock below the place of the Lord's Cross, where there is an altar on which the Sacrifice is offered for the souls of certain privileged men.

SCRIPTURE READINGS: GOLGOTHA

Luke 23:33–47 (The crucifixion of Jesus): When they came to the place that is called The Skull, they crucified Jesus there with the criminals, one on his right and one on his left. Then Jesus said, "Father, forgive them; for they do not know what they are doing." And they cast lots to divide his clothing. And the people stood by, watching; but the leaders scoffed at him, saying, "He saved others; let him save himself if he is the Messiah of God, his chosen one!" The soldiers also mocked him, coming up and offering him sour wine, and saying, "If you are the King of the Jews, save yourself!" There was also an inscription over him, "This is the King of the Jews."

    One of the criminals who were hanged there kept deriding him and saying, "Are you not the Messiah? Save yourself and us!" But the other rebuked him, saying, "Do you not fear God, since you are under the same sentence of condemnation? And we indeed have been condemned justly, for we are getting what we deserve for our deeds, but this man has done nothing wrong." Then he said, "Jesus, remember me when you come into your kingdom." He replied, "Truly I tell you, today you will be with me in Paradise." It was now about noon, and darkness came over the whole land until three in the afternoon, while the sun's light failed; and the curtain of the temple was torn in two. Then Jesus, crying with a loud voice, said, "Father, into your hands I commend my spirit." Having said this, he breathed his last. When the centurion saw what had taken place, he praised God and said, "Certainly this man was innocent."

John 19:16–30 (The crucifixion of Jesus): So they took Jesus; and carrying the cross by himself, he went out to what is called The Place of the Skull, which in Hebrew is called Golgotha. There they crucified him, and with him two others, one on either side, with Jesus between them. Pilate also had an inscription written and put on the cross. It read, "Jesus of Nazareth, the King of the Jews." Many of the Jews read this inscription, because the place where Jesus was crucified was near the city; and it was written in Hebrew, in Latin, and in Greek. Then the chief priests of the Jews said to Pilate, "Do not write, 'The King of the Jews,' but, 'This man said, I am King of the Jews.'" Pilate answered, "What I have written I have written." When the soldiers had crucified Jesus, they took his clothes and divided them into four parts, one for each soldier. They also took his tunic; now the tunic was seamless, woven in one piece from the top. So they said to one another, "Let us not tear it, but cast lots for it to see who will get it." This was to fulfill what the scripture says, "They divided my clothes among themselves, and for my clothing they cast lots." And that is what the soldiers did.

Meanwhile, standing near the cross of Jesus were his mother, and his mother's sister, Mary the wife of Clopas, and Mary Magdalene. When Jesus saw his mother and the disciple whom he loved standing beside her, he said to his mother, "Woman, here is your son." Then he said to the disciple, "Here is your mother." And from that hour the disciple took her into his own home. After this, when Jesus knew that all was now finished, he said (in order to fulfill the scripture), "I am thirsty." A jar full of sour wine was standing there. So they put a sponge full of the wine on a branch of hyssop and held it to his mouth. When Jesus had received the wine, he said, "It is finished." Then he bowed his head and gave up his spirit.

Genesis 22:1–18 (The command to sacrifice Isaac): After these things God tested Abraham. He said to him, "Abraham!" And he said, "Here I am." He said, "Take your son, your only son Isaac, whom you love, and go to the land of Moriah, and offer him there as a burnt offering on one of the mountains that I shall show you." So Abraham rose early in the morning, saddled his donkey, and took two of his young men with him, and his son Isaac; he cut the wood for the burnt offering, and set out and went to the place in the distance that God had shown him. On the third day Abraham looked up and saw the place far away. Then Abraham said to his young men, "Stay here with the donkey; the boy and I will go over there; we will worship, and then we will come back to you." Abraham took the wood of the burnt offering and laid it on his son Isaac, and he himself carried the fire and the knife. So the two of them walked on together. Isaac said to his father Abraham, "Father!" And he said, "Here I am, my son." He said, "The fire and the wood are here, but where is the lamb for a burnt offering?" Abraham said, "God himself will provide the lamb for a burnt offering, my son." So the two of them walked on together.

When they came to the place that God had shown him, Abraham built an altar there and laid the wood in order. He bound his son Isaac, and laid him on the altar, on top of the wood. Then Abraham reached out his hand and took the knife to kill his son. But the angel of the Lord called to him from heaven, and said, "Abraham, Abraham!" And he said, "Here I am." He said, "Do not lay your hand on the boy or do anything to him; for now I know that you fear God, since you have not withheld your son, your only son, from me." And Abraham looked up and saw a ram, caught in a thicket by its horns. Abraham went and took the ram and offered it up as a burnt offering instead of his son. So Abraham called that place "The Lord will provide"; as it is said to this day, "On the mount of the Lord it shall be provided."

The angel of the Lord called to Abraham a second time from heaven, and said, "By myself I have sworn, says the Lord: Because you have done this, and have not withheld your son, your only son, I will indeed bless you, and I will make your offspring as numerous as the stars of heaven and as the sand that is on the seashore. And your offspring shall possess the gate of their enemies, and by your offspring shall all the nations of the earth gain blessing for themselves, because you have obeyed my voice."

COMMEMORATING STATION 2: THE TOMB OF ADAM

- Take the opposite set of steps to the tomb of Adam (the Chapel of Adam), which is underneath the upper chapels.
- Read the background information, pilgrimage texts, and Scripture readings for the tomb of Adam.
- Why does Adam warrant recognition in the Holy Sepulchre? How is Jesus like and not like a second Adam?
- Look at the exposed sections of the rock of Calvary both inside and outside the chapel. How does the rejected stone inform the commemoration of Jesus' crucifixion?
- Study the large wall mosaic of the crucifixion, anointing, and entombment of Jesus outside the Chapel of Adam behind the stone of anointing. What details strike you? What emotions does it elicit?
- Observe pilgrims at the stone of anointing. Interact with it, as you wish.
- End in prayer.

BACKGROUND INFORMATION: THE TOMB OF ADAM

Intriguingly, the exegetical idea that Adam was buried beneath the place of Jesus' crucifixion precedes the construction of the Holy Sepulchre with the earliest known mention coming from Origen (d. c. 253), who wrote a century before the fourth-century development of the site.[20] Although the tomb of Adam is a *theological* commemoration, the idea embraces a literal concept of physical atonement: the blood of Jesus, the second Adam, dripped on the bones of the first Adam, thereby atoning for original sin and redeeming humanity. The skull and crossbones at the bottom of crucifixes and depictions of the cross represent mortality and human sin; specifically, they are the bones of Adam (see the wall mosaic outside the chapel).

Although there is no actual tomb, the lower chapel is dedicated to Adam's resting place at the base of Golgotha. The rock pillar can be seen

20. Origen, *Commentary on St. Matthew* 27.32–33.

both inside and outside the chapel with the section in the corridor particularly evocative: the dark orange coloring in the rock is suggestive to some of the blood of Christ.

Espoused by Jerome and followed by the pilgrim writers Adomnán and Bede, there was an alternative tradition that Adam was buried in Hebron with the three patriarchs, Abraham, Isaac, and Jacob.[21] This was partly driven by the fact that the Hebrew name for Hebron is Kiryat Arba, or the "village of four" (see Gen 23:2). Early scholars speculated on the fourth person, with candidates also including Caleb and Joseph.

Greeting pilgrims as they enter the Holy Sepulchre, the large wall mosaic of Jesus' passion (1990) serves as a backdrop for the popular stone of anointing, or stone of unction, a station that postdates the Circuit.[22] A devotional focal point for modern-day pilgrims, the stone commemorates the anointing of Jesus' body after he was taken down from the cross. According to John 19:38–40, Joseph of Arimathea prepared Jesus' body with a mixture of oils and spices and wrapped the body in cloth before placing it in the tomb. Today, pilgrims pour oil on the horizontal slab of rock as they kneel in prayer and trace their fingers on the stone. Their tactile prayers are driven by the thought that they are touching an object that has had physical contact with the body of Christ. Although the current stone has only been in place since 1810, pilgrim imitation of Joseph's devotion, the emotional intimacy of anointing Jesus' body for burial, and the sense of latent resurrection that inhabits the station make it one of the most spiritually poignant settings in the Holy Land.

The stone of anointing is also a place for blessing the physical accoutrements of the journey: items acquired in the Holy Land as well as those brought from home. Pilgrims place objects on the rock, like crosses, icons, and rosaries, which are prayed over, dedicated, and taken home as sacred mementos. Orthodox pilgrims, in particular, anoint white gowns to be worn as resurrection garments after their death, thus, preparing their burial clothes where Jesus' body was likewise prepared for burial. Many of these same gowns have been previously worn in the Jordan River, following a pre-Crusader tradition of turning baptism clothes into burial gowns. The Piacenza Pilgrim observed in the sixth century that pilgrims "all go down

---

21. On the tradition of Adam's burial in Hebron, see Jerome, *Hebrew Questions on Genesis* 23.2; Adomnán, *On the Holy Places* 2.9–10; Bede, *On the Holy Places* 8.

22. In the late Middle Ages, the stone of unction was outside in the southern courtyard (parvis).

into the Jordan River for a blessing dressed in linen and many other materials that they will keep for their own burial."[23]

PILGRIMAGE TEXTS: THE TOMB OF ADAM

***The Armenian Guide* 3 (c. 630):** Ten paces away from "The Resurrection" is the holy Church of Golgotha. It is called "The Tomb of Adam" below, and above there is an altar. On its rock Christ was crucified.

Epiphanius, *Holy City* 2 (before 692): And in the middle of the Holy City is the holy Tomb of the Lord, and near the Tomb the Place of the Skull. There Christ was crucified. Its height is thirty-two steps. And beneath the Crucifixion there is a church, the Tomb of Adam.

SCRIPTURE READINGS: THE TOMB OF ADAM

Romans 5:12–14 (also see vv. 15–21): Therefore, just as sin came into the world through one man, and death came through sin, and so death spread to all because all have sinned—sin was indeed in the world before the law, but sin is not reckoned when there is no law. Yet death exercised dominion from Adam to Moses, even over those whose sins were not like the transgression of Adam, who is a type of the one who was to come.

1 Corinthians 15:20–22: But in fact Christ has been raised from the dead, the first fruits of those who have died. For since death came through a human being, the resurrection of the dead has also come through a human being; for as all die in Adam, so all will be made alive in Christ.

---

23. Piacenza Pilgrim, *Travels* 11.

Station 3
The Holy Cross

THE STATION

The Chapel of the Finding of the Cross. Exit the Chapel of Adam, keeping the area of Golgotha on your right. In the semicircular ambulatory, descend the staircase on the right, noting the crosses carved by medieval pilgrims on the walls. At the base of the stairs, continue ahead on the right, and proceed down another set of steps to the quarried chapel below.

Fig. 11. Jerusalem, 1158. Bayerische Staatsbibliothek München, Clm 13002, fol. 4v. Twelfth-century drawing accompanying the text of Bede, *De locis sanctis* (c. 702), which incorporates the description of the column of the miraculous healing of the Holy Cross in Adomnán, *De locis sanctis* 1.11, written in the late seventh century. The column also marked the center of the world. Used with permission.

COMMEMORATING STATION 3: THE HOLY CROSS

In the Franciscan Chapel of the Finding of the Cross:

- Begin in prayer.
- Read the background information and the pilgrimage texts for the Holy Cross.
- Observe the statue of St. Helena holding the cross. Donated by the Austro-Hungarian prince Maximilian, who later became the king of Mexico, it was erected in 1857 and restored in 1965.
- Why has the cross, an instrument of death by execution, become associated with healing? Reflect on the phrase: "the power of the cross."
- Observe signs of the ancient quarry around you. See how workers cut underneath the upper rock to remove better stone. Reflect on the metaphor of levels and layers. Are there contexts in life in which it is wise to leave behind the lesser and go deeper to access more quality substance?
- Locate the Crusader wall designs behind the glass.
- Light a candle, if you wish.
- End in prayer.

BACKGROUND INFORMATION: THE HOLY CROSS

In the pre-Crusader period, the finding of the Holy Cross was essentially on par with Golgotha and the tomb of Christ, especially as a place of prayer, healing, and miracles. Helena's alleged role in discovering the True Cross was a "central fact" of Jerusalem pilgrimage, and pilgrims came to the Holy Sepulchre to venerate all three places (note: the terms Holy Cross and True Cross are interchangeable, as well as the words *finding*, *discovery*, and *invention*).

Comprised of two events—the invention of the three crosses and a subsequent healing—the legend of the Holy Cross can be summarized as follows: Helena went to Jerusalem to search for the holy places. When she inquired about the place of the crucifixion, she learned that it was covered by a Roman temple. Upon subsequently removing the temple, three crosses were discovered, but there was no way to identify the True Cross from

The Stations

those of the thieves. Helena subsequently applied the crosses to a mortally sick or dead woman, and as the True Cross touched the woman, she was miraculously healed. In the Western version, the sick person is generally a young man already deceased. Again, the legend consists of two distinct events: Helena's discovery of the three crosses and a miraculous healing that identified which one was the True Cross of Christ.[24]

The *finding* of the True Cross was originally commemorated in the apse of the Basilica of Constantine, which corresponds to an area west of the Crusader ambulatory (inside the Greek Katholicon). After the destruction of the basilica, the commemoration was moved to its present location in the crypt, which was opened up in the twelfth century (no pre-Crusader sources mention a crypt). The *miraculous healing* was commemorated in an exedra near Golgotha in the Byzantine period,[25] before a purpose-built column dedicated to the miraculous healing was erected at the northeast corner of the complex close to the western cardo, likely in the wake of the restoration of the Holy Cross by Heraclius in 630.[26] Also of interest is Adomnán's drawing of the Holy Sepulchre which depicts three crosses inside the basilica (fig. 6), while Willibald describes three large wooden crosses outside the eastern end of the basilica that were previously inside the church.[27]

Moving from places and memories to physical objects, the Holy Cross was a featured relic of the Holy Sepulchre throughout the Byzantine period before being transferred to Constantinople in the seventh century. Egeria (380s) provides a colorful account of the relic's veneration on Good Friday:

> So, when [the relic] has been placed on the table, the bishop, sitting, grips the ends of the holy wood with his hands, and the deacons who stand around guard it. It is guarded thus because the custom is that all the people coming one by one, both the faithful and the catechumens, bowing at the table, kiss the holy wood and pass through. And because, I don't know when, someone is said to have bitten off and stolen a piece of the holy wood, therefore it is now thus guarded by the deacons who stand around lest anyone dares to come and do so again.[28]

24. See Borgehammar, *How the Holy Cross Was Found*.

25. *Breviarius* B, c.

26. See Aist, "Monument of the Miraculous Healing"; Aist, *Christian Topography*, 63–106; Aist, *From Topography to Text*, discussed throughout.

27. Hugeburc, *Life of Willibald* 18.

28. Egeria, *Travels* 37.2 (from McGowan and Bradshaw). A splinter relic is kept today

Relics of the Holy Cross are well attested in the fourth century, both in Jerusalem and beyond, and prior to 350, Cyril of Jerusalem could already state that the whole world was filled with fragments of the wood![29] However, the first extant source linking Helena with the Holy Cross is the funeral oration, *On the Death of Theodosius*, by Ambrose of Milan, which does not occur until 395. Although Eusebius confirms Helena's role in founding Holy Land churches, namely, the Church of the Nativity and the Eleona, there is reason to question her involvement in the discovery of the relics—conclusively so if her sojourn in Jerusalem occurred in 328 after the Roman temple had already been removed and construction of the Holy Sepulchre had begun.[30]

The feast of the finding of the Holy Cross is September 14, which was originally the second day of an eight-day festival commemorating the dedication of the Holy Sepulchre. The festival was the setting for the conversion of Mary the Egyptian (see below).

PILGRIMAGE TEXTS: THE HOLY CROSS

The Piacenza Pilgrim, *Travels* 20 (c. 570): From Golgotha there are 50 steps to where the Cross was discovered in the Basilica of Constantine, which adjoins the Tomb and Golgotha. In the atrium of this basilica is a small room, where the Wood of the Cross is kept, which we venerated and kissed. Now the title, which was placed at the head of the Lord, in which was written, "Here is the King of the Jews"—I held it in my hand and kissed it. The Wood of the Cross is from the nut tree. At the same hour as the Holy Cross is brought out from its room to be venerated in the atrium, a star appears in the sky and comes above the place where the Cross has been placed, and while the Cross is venerated, the star remains above it, and oil is offered for a blessing in small ampullas. When the mouth of the small ampullas touches the Wood of the Cross, the oil soon bubbles up, and if the ampulla is not quickly closed, it causes the oil to overflow. When the Cross is taken back to its place, the star also returns: after the Cross has been put back, the star no longer appears. There is also the sponge and the reed, which one reads about in the Gospel, and we drank water from the sponge. And there is the onyx chalice which he blessed at the Lord's Supper, and many other marvelous things: an image of Blessed Mary in a high place, her

---

in the Greek treasury adjacent to the Chapel of Adam.

29. Cyril of Jerusalem, *Catechesis* 4.10.
30. See Hillner, *Helena Augusta*, 204–44.

The Stations

girdle, and the band that she used to wear on her head. And there are seven marble seats of the elders.

***Breviarius* A, b (c. 525):** From there you go into the Church of St. Constantine. The great apse to the west is the place where the three crosses were found.

***Breviarius* B, c (c. 525):** And then going into Golgotha . . . there is an exedra at the place where the man was brought back to life and proved which was the Cross of Christ, and this Cross is adorned with gold and gems, with a golden dome about it.

Sophronius, *Anacreontica* 20.35–38 (before 614): Exultant let me go on to the place where all of us who belong to the people of God venerate the glorious Wood of the Cross.

Adomnán (Arculf), *On the Holy Places* 1.11 (680s): Something must be said of a very tall column which stands in the middle of the city, to the north of the holy places, where it is seen by every passer-by. This column was set up at the place where the Lord's Cross was placed on a dead young man, and he came to life.

Epiphanius, *Holy Place* 4 (before 692): And on the left side of [the Basilica of Constantine] is the house of Joseph. And below the house there is a structure with four columns in which Saint Helena met the funeral procession of the maiden. The maiden was placed against the three crosses, and spoke when it was the Cross of the Lord.

Hugeburc (Willibald), *Life of Willibald* 18, 25 (724–26): From there [Willibald] came on to Jerusalem, to the place where the Lord's Holy Cross was found. That place is called "The Place of Calvary" and there is now a church there: in earlier times it was outside Jerusalem, but Helena put the place inside Jerusalem when she found the Cross. Now there are three wooden crosses standing there outside the church, on the east of it near the wall, to commemorate the Holy Cross of the Lord, and those of the others who were crucified with him. Nowadays they are not indoors, inside the church, but stand out of doors under a roof outside the church. . . . [He] returned once again to Jerusalem. As he entered the church where the Holy Cross was discovered, his eyes were opened and he recovered his sight.

Crusader Text: Daniel the Abbot, *Pilgrimage of Daniel the Monk* **15 (1106–8):** Here is the place where St. Helena found the True Cross near the place of the Lord's crucifixion, 20 fathoms farther to the east. And on that spot a very large square church (dedicated to the Exaltation of the True Cross) was built, but now there is only a small church. . . . And near this door is the place where St. Helena discovered the true cross of the Lord, instantly restoring a dead virgin to life.

Station 4
The Center of the World

THE STATION

The Katholicon, the primary Greek liturgical space directly opposite the aedicule, contains a small pedestal about two feet high that marks the center of the world. Only a few meters inside the room, the marker is the middle of the floor adjacent to an offering box. When the Katholicon is closed off by a chain, it is still possible to see the pedestal; occasionally the view is obstructed by a curtain.

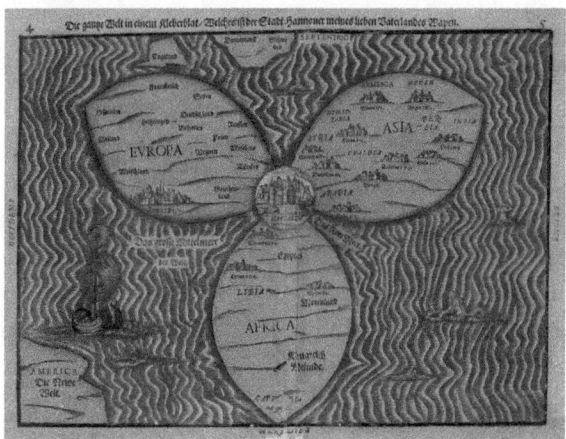

Fig. 12. The Bünting Cloverleaf Map, 1585. Map showing Europe, Asia, and Africa in the form of a clover leaf with Jerusalem in the center. Heinrich Bünting (German, 1545–1606). Woodcut. Eran Laor Map Collection. The National Library of Israel. Public domain.

COMMEMORATING STATION 4: THE CENTER OF THE WORD

From inside the Katholicon or near the entrance:

- Begin in prayer.
- Read the background information, pilgrimage texts, and Scripture readings for the center of the world.
- Reflect on the death and resurrection of Jesus as the "center point" of the Christian faith.
- Consider the idea of the Holy Sepulchre as the center of the world in Christian tradition. How is it true? In what ways is it a misconception?
- How is Jerusalem the center of the world for the Abrahamic faiths? How is the city a gathering place for each of the three religions?
- Why is Jerusalem a focal point for contemporary global politics?
- Reflect on the spirituality of *middles and centers* and *edges and margins* as it applies to individuals, communities, and societies. How is the spirituality of the edges (e.g., margins, boundaries, and borders) different from that of the center? How is life/God/power perceived from the center? What is life/God/power like on the margins?
- If the Katholicon is open, approach the center of the world. Touch it; measure it. Take a photo with it.
- Observe the Katholicon in detail. Note the image of Christ in the dome.
- The area of the Katholicon was formerly an open courtyard of the Byzantine complex; the dome was added during the Crusader period. Imagine the space open to the sky without the dome. Look in the direction of the Golgotha chapels, which were originally visible from the courtyard. Recalling the sequence of Jesus' crucifixion, entombment, and resurrection, trace with an imaginative eye the movement of Jesus' body from Golgotha to the tomb.
- End in prayer.

The Stations

BACKGROUND INFORMATION: THE CENTER OF THE WORLD

Appropriating Jewish thought concerning the temple, Christian tradition has recognized the Holy Sepulchre as the center of the world. More than a geographical center, in each instance, the designation denotes an omphalos, or navel, that serves as the life-giving source of the world. Medieval Christian tradition added the incorrect claim—true for the Tropic of Cancer—that there was no shadow in Jerusalem at noon day on the summer solstice, further "proving" that the city was the center of the world.

Notwithstanding the concept of the navel, the Christian appeal to the center of the world stems from the events of salvation that occurred there—Jesus' death and resurrection—rather than an ontological argument for the sacredness of the place itself. Adhering to the doctrine of God's universal presence, Christianity has never promulgated an argument for qualitatively distinct sacred places. Christians may speak of holy, sacred, or thin places—as well as the center of the world—but these are not doctrinal claims that certain places are intrinsically holy or qualitatively distinct. A place may be suggestive, made special by events, or consecrated by prayer, but God is equally and universally present. Likewise, with respect to the Holy Sepulchre, the commemoration of the center of the world appeals to biblical history and the events of salvation, not to the idea that the area was *created* holy.

We are dealing instead with how religious imagination seeks biblical connections through commemorative ideas. The assertion that once every year Jerusalem was a shadowless city—and thus at the center of the world—should be understood in terms of Christian associations of the earthly city with biblical descriptions of New Jerusalem. From Eusebius on down, Christians viewed the city and, in particular, the Holy Sepulchre as a New Jerusalem made of stone. As described in Rev 21–22, Jerusalem was a city without a temple containing the throne of the Lamb of God, understood as the tomb of Christ. A manifestation of New Jerusalem, the lack of shadows on the summer solstice "foreshadowed" the time when the city would have no need for either the sun or the moon as God's glory would shine all around (Rev 21:23–25).

The center of the world has been visually and physically expressed in pilgrim tradition. On the Madaba Map, the monumental entrance of the Holy Sepulchre is at the very center of Jerusalem, while Jerusalem, in turn, marks the middle of the map. The Holy City is commonly depicted as the center of the world in later maps (see fig. 12). In the Holy Sepulchre itself, the center of the world has been commemorated in various ways and locations. Sophronius (c. 614) locates it at Golgotha; Arculf (680s) links it with a tall column near the eastern entrance of the complex, while Nikulás of þverá (c. 1140) associates it with the open dome above Christ's tomb. Bernard (870) describes the intersection of chains in the inner courtyard as the center of the world, which corresponds to the area of the Katholicon, where it's commemorated today.

As previously stated, the Katholicon was formerly the inner courtyard of the Byzantine complex and was open to the sky. Though paved with marble, the courtyard served as a commemorative garden between Golgotha and the tomb of Christ (John 19:41), and from the middle of the courtyard, one could see both sites: the upper chapel of Golgotha in the southeast corner of the courtyard and the tomb directly to the west. Following the destruction of the complex in 1009, the courtyard was roofed by the Crusaders, which accounts for the second dome.

PILGRIMAGE TEXTS: THE CENTER OF THE WORLD

Sophronius, *Anacreontica* 20.29–32 (before 614): And prostrate I will venerate the Navel-point of the earth, that divine Rock in which was fixed the Wood which undid the curse of the tree.

Adomnán (Arculf), *On the Holy Places* 1.11 (680s): A summary account must be given of a very high column which stands in the centre of the city to the north of the holy places facing the passers-by. It is remarkable how this column (which is situated in the place where the dead youth came to life when the cross of the Lord was placed upon him) fails to cast a shadow at midday during the Summer solstice, when the sun reaches the centre of the heavens. When the solstice is passed, however (that is the 8th day before the kalends of July), after an interval of three days, as the day gradually grows shorter it casts a brief shadow at first, then as the days pass a longer one. And so this column, which the sunlight surrounds on all sides blazing directly down on it during the midday hours (when at the Summer solstice the sun stands in the centre of the heavens), proves Jerusalem to be situated at the centre of the world. Hence the psalmist, because of the holy places of the passion and resurrection, which are contained within Helia itself, prophesying sings: "God our king before the ages hath wrought our salvation in the centre of the earth," that is Jerusalem, which is said to be in the centre of the earth and its navel (trans. Meehan).

Bernard, *Journey to the Holy Places* 11 (870): Amongst the churches inside the city there are four of special importance, and their walls adjoin each other. One is on the east, and inside it are Mount Calvary and the place where the Lord's Cross was found; this one is called "The Basilica of Constantine." There is another one on the south and a third on the west: this one has the Lord's Sepulchre in the middle of it. . . . Furthermore these four churches have between them a garden without a roof, with its walls sparkling with gold and a paved floor of the costliest stone. From each of the four churches runs a chain, and the point at which the four chains join in the centre of this garden is said to be the centre of the world.

Crusader Text: Saewulf, *Pilgrimage of Saewulf* 12 (1101–3): Outside the Church of the Holy Sepulchre but within its surrounding walls, not far from the place of Calvary, in the place called "Compass," where our Lord Jesus Christ with his own hand marked and measured the centre of the world, as the Psalmist bears witness: "But the Lord our King has before the ages worked salvation in the centre of the earth."

Crusader Text: Nikulás of þverá, *Extract* 84–86 (c. 1140): It is called the Church of the Holy Sepulchre and it is open above over the sepulchre. The center of the earth is there, where the sun shines directly down from the sky on the feast of John.[31]

SCRIPTURE READINGS:
THE CENTER OF THE WORLD

Psalm 74:12: Yet God my King is from of old, working salvation in [the midst of] the earth.

Ezekiel 5:5: Thus says the Lord God: This is Jerusalem; I have set her in the center of the nations, with countries all around her.

Ezekiel 38:12: And the people who were gathered from the nations . . . who live at the center of the earth.

---
31. The summer solstice was previously on June 24, the feast of St. John.

Station 5
Mary the Egyptian

THE STATION

The conversion of Mary the Egyptian occurred near the eastern façade of the Basilica of Constantine. Following the destruction of the basilica in 1009, the primary entrance to the Holy Sepulchre moved to the south bringing the commemoration with it. Today, the Chapel of Mary the Egyptian is in the southern courtyard (parvis) of the Holy Sepulchre underneath the large set of outdoor steps that formerly gave access to Golgotha. The disused chapel, which is never open, has a light gray metal door.

Fig. 13. *S. Marie Egyptienne* (St. Mary of Egypt), April 2nd, from "Les Images De Tous Les Saincts et Saintes de L'Année," published 1636. Jacques Callot (French, 1592–1635). Etching. The Metropolitan Museum of Art. Open Access. Public domain.

The Stations

COMMEMORATING STATION 5: MARY THE EGYPTIAN

You may choose to commemorate the station nearer its original setting. Between the eighth and ninth stations of the Via Dolorosa, the Way of the Cross leaves Khan ez-Zeit Street (the western cardo) via two flights of steps. At the top of the steps, turn left with the lane and continue to the dark green door in the north-south wall straight ahead. Although the wall is *not* aligned with the façade of the Constantinian basilica, it offers an appropriate visual marker to remember the conversion of Mary of Egypt in the immediate vicinity of its original location. You can also get there via the Ethiopian chapels (adjacent to the Chapel of Mary the Egyptian) in the northeast corner of the parvis of the Holy Sepulchre; once back outside, go through the opposite doorway: the suggested location is around the corner from the ninth station. At either location:

- Begin in prayer.
- Read the background information and pilgrimage texts, including excerpts from *The Life of Mary the Egyptian*.
- What reactions do you have to the story?
- Reflect upon the Holy Sepulchre as a place of personal repentance.
- How is the Holy Sepulchre a place of encounter that sends Christians out "into the world" with a new identity, vocation, or commitment?
- End in prayer.

BACKGROUND INFORMATION: MARY THE EGYPTIAN

No medieval pilgrim would have visited the Holy Sepulchre without encountering the story of Mary the Egyptian, a desert mother from the fifth or sixth century. The primary source for her life is the seventh-century text *The Life of Mary the Egyptian*, written by the same Sophronius, the patriarch of Jerusalem, who wrote the *Anacreontica*. According to her *Life*, Mary the Egyptian was a prostitute who came to Jerusalem in the company of pilgrims for the September feast of the Holy Cross, which was part of the annual festival of the dedication of the Holy Sepulchre. While attempting to enter the church, an invisible force held her back until she repented of her lifestyle to an icon of the Theotokos hanging on or near the basilica façade. Mary was then allowed to enter the church to venerate the Holy Cross. Upon returning to the icon, she was instructed to go to the desert beyond the Jordan River where she would find peace.

Mary lived as a desert mother in the Jordan River Valley for forty-seven years. Near the end of her life, now old and emaciated, she was found by a priest named Zosimos. After telling Zosimos her story, her one request was to be given Eucharist on Holy Thursday. After Zosimos fulfilled her wish, she asked to meet again the following year. When he returned the subsequent Holy Thursday, he found Mary's deceased body. According to a message written in the sand, she died on the night he gave her Holy Communion the previous year.

PILGRIMAGE TEXTS: MARY THE EGYPTIAN

Epiphanius, *Holy City* **4 (before 692):** And on the left side of Saint Constantine is the icon of the very holy Theotokos, who forbade Saint Mary to enter the church on the day of the Exaltation. There also she made her promise.

Crusader Source: Daniel the Abbot, *Pilgrimage of Daniel the Monk* **15 (1106–8):** Here to the East is the great door to which came St. Mary the Egyptian desiring to enter and kiss [the cross], but the power of the Holy Spirit would not admit her to the church. And then she prayed to the Holy Mother of God whose ikon was in the porch near the door, and then she was able to enter the church and kiss the True Cross. By this door she went out again into the desert of the Jordan.

Sophronius, excerpts from *The Life of Mary the Egyptian* **(before 638):** Finally, we arrived in Jerusalem. In the days before the festival, I spent my time in the city living the same kind of life as before. When the hour of the elevation of the Holy Cross approached, I made my way with the great crowds to enter the church. But as I came to the doorstep that everyone passed, I was prevented from entering by an unknown force. I tried to elbow my way forward, but I struggled in vain. I alone remained behind, unreceived by the church. I repeated my efforts, at least three or four times, until at last I became exhausted. So, I stepped aside to the corner of the porch. It was only then that I began to understand why I was being prevented from

The Stations

seeing the lifegiving relic of the True Cross. The word of God's salvation slowly touched my heart and revealed to me that my impure life had kept me from entering the church. I began to weep and lament and to sigh with groans from my heart. And then as I stood sobbing, I saw above me the icon of the most holy Theotokos, and casting my physical and spiritual eyes upon her, I said:

> Dear Mother of God, who gave birth to God incarnate, there is no honor or praise to you when one so depraved and impure as I gaze at your image. I rightly inspire hatred and disgust before your purity, but I have heard that God who was born of you became man for the purpose of calling sinners to repentance. Then help me, for I have no other help. Order the church to be opened to me. Allow me to see the holy tree on which the one born to you suffered in the flesh and shed his holy blood for the redemption of sinners and for me, unworthy as I am. Be my witness before your son that I will never again defile my body, but as soon as I have seen the Holy Cross I will renounce the world and its temptations, and I will go wherever you lead me.

I left the spot where I was praying and once again mingled with the crowd that was pushing its way into the church. I was now able to enter the holy place without constraints. I saw the lifegiving Cross, and I saw too the mysterious nature of God and how the Lord accepts repentance. Prostrating myself on the ground, I kissed the earth with my tears. When I came out from the church, I went back to her who had helped redeem me, to the place where I had sealed my vow. And on bended knee before the Theotokos, I said, "O loving Virgin Mother of God, you have shown me your great love. Now lead me on the path of repentance!" And with these words, a voice spoke from on high: "If you cross the Jordan, you will find peace."

I left the church and set off on my journey. It was sunset when I reached the Church of St. John the Baptist on the banks of the Jordan. After praying in the church, I went down to the Jordan, rinsed my hands and face in the river, and drank some of the holy water. Then I lay down, passing the night on the ground. The next morning, I found a small boat and crossed over to the opposite side.[32]

---

32. A paraphrase of selections from the text. For the full text from the Internet Medieval Sourcebook, see https://sourcebooks.fordham.edu/basis/maryegypt.asp.

Stations 6–7
The Church of Holy Sion

DIRECTIONS:
THE HOLY SEPULCHRE TO HOLY SION

As you leave the Holy Sepulchre, exit the courtyard through an arch in the far-left corner. Keeping buildings on your left, continue until you reach the four-way intersection of Suq ed-Dabbagha and al-Attarin Street (Khan ez-Zeit). Here, the western cardo runs left to right (north to south). Turn right on al-Attarin Street, and continue down the length of the lane until you come to the Jewish Quarter, where its name changes to Cardo Street. Walk as far as you can on Cardo Street before eventually taking the parallel street on the left, Jewish Quarter Street. Continue straight in the same direction (south) until you come to a parking lot. Immediately before the parking lot, take the sidewalk on the right (Tif'eret Yerushalayim Street), which soon ends at a T-junction. Turn left on Habad Street, continuing along the edge of the parking lot in the direction of the city walls. Follow the sidewalk as it turns right around the corner; the tarmac road parallel on the left is Sion Gate Street. Take the street for a short distance until you come to Sion Gate, which is on the left. Cross the road and pass through the gate, exiting the Old City.

Upon leaving the Old City, continue straight on a sidewalk, keeping the parking lot on your left and the wall of the St. Savior Armenian Monastery on your right. At the end of the parking lot—just before a Franciscan monastery—the sidewalk veers to the right. Take the lane a short distance to the angled corner of the Dormition Abbey. The left fork takes you to the

Cenacle; the door is on the left. The right fork leads to the courtyard of the Dormition Abbey.

THE STATIONS OF HOLY SION

The area of the former Church of Holy Sion on the summit of the Western Hill (Mount Sion) is divided into two stations: the Cenacle, commemorating the Last Supper and Pentecost (station 6) and the Dormition Abbey, remembering the death of Mary (station 7). The stations can be done in either order.

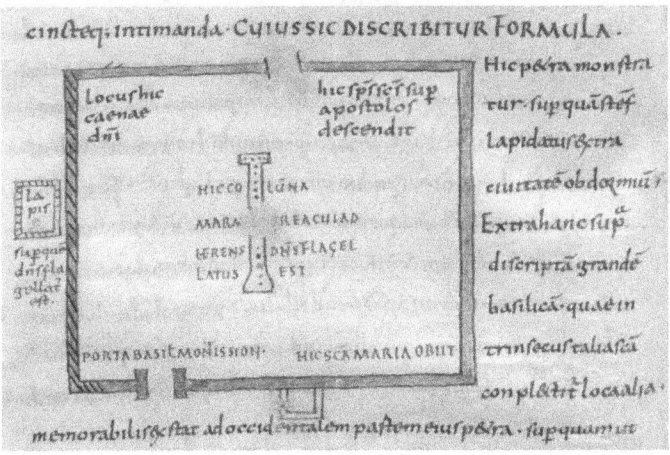

Fig. 14. The Church of Holy Sion. Vienna, Österreichische Nationalbibliothek, Cod. 458, fol. 9v. Ninth-century manuscript drawing based on the late seventh-century prototype in Adomnán, *De locis sanctis*. Used with permission.

Key to the drawing (the top is south):

- Upper left (southeast): Here is the place of the Lord's Supper.
- Upper right (southwest): Here is where the Holy Spirit descended upon the disciples.
- Bottom left (northeast): The door of the Basilica of Mount Sion.
- Bottom right (northwest): Here Saint Mary died.
- Center: Here stands the marble column to which the Lord cleaved when he was scourged.
- Left side chapel (east): The rock upon which the Lord was scourged.

BACKGROUND INFORMATION: HOLY SION

To clarify terms: the name of the *mountain* is Mount Sion, identified as the southern end of the Western Hill. The name of the Byzantine *church* on Mount Sion was Holy Sion; the Crusader church was dedicated to Mary. It is important to understand that the place-name Sion has moved from its original location. The "stronghold of Zion" that David captured from the Jebusites was on the Eastern Hill, identified as "the city of David" (2 Sam 5:7). Elsewhere in the Old Testament, Sion denotes the temple on the upper Eastern Hill, while it is also equated with Jerusalem as whole. By the late Old Testament period, Jerusalem had expanded to the Western Hill, which is significantly higher than the eastern one. Given the biblical attributes of Sion—stronghold, holy mountain, high, great, and mighty—it became a logical, if inevitable, step to identify Sion with the highest summit in the city. By the late Second Temple period, the name had been transferred to the Western Hill.[33] While there are no topographical references to Mount Sion in the New Testament (it appears as a metaphor), the connection between Sion and the Western Hill would be fully developed in the Christian period.

The relationship between the Western Hill (Mount Sion) and the city walls is also confusing. The area was *inside* the city during the time of Jesus. The line of the southern walls receded to the north after the fall of the temple—leaving the summit of Mount Sion *outside* the walls—where they remained throughout the late Roman and early Byzantine periods until the mid-fifth century when the Empress Eudocia (d. 460) restored the extended line of the walls bringing the southern end of the Western Hill back into the city and, with it, the Byzantine Church of Holy Sion. The church's intramural location can be seen on the Madaba Map (c. 600). Following an earthquake in 1033, the southern extension was abandoned to where the south walls stand today. The Circuit focuses on the New Testament period and the three centuries between the Sophronius text (c. 614) and the travels of Bernard the Monk (870). During both eras, Mount Sion (the Western Hill) was inside the city.

Fourth-century references to Mount Sion include the statement of the Bordeaux Pilgrim (333) that of seven former synagogues only one was left, while Epiphanius of Salamis (d. 403) retrospectively writes in 392 that in the second-century days of Hadrian there were seven synagogues and "a

---

33. See Josephus, *Jewish War* 5.137; Magness, *Jerusalem*, 361.

little church of God."[34] It's uncertain whether either the church or synagogue were related to (or located on) the subsequent Byzantine site. By tradition, the Church of Holy Sion, constructed before 348, incorporated the place where the disciples gathered before and after the resurrection,[35] but the early fourth-century evidence, including what preceded the Byzantine church, is unclear.

In the Byzantine period, the church's subsequent commemorations—Pentecost, the Last Supper, and the death of Mary—testify to the understanding of Holy Sion as the center of the New Testament church. Of the three, Pentecost is the earliest memory. Due to its apostolic associations, including the tradition that James the Just, the brother of Jesus and the first bishop of Jerusalem, was consecrated there, Holy Sion was known as "the mother of all churches." Its prominence is depicted on the Madaba Map. In short, while the Holy Sepulchre was the place of Jesus' death and resurrection, Holy Sion was the church of the apostles. It was an important venue of the stational liturgy of Jerusalem as well as the catechetical lectures of Cyril of Jerusalem (d. 386). Holy Sion was also a repository of sacred relics, including objects that had no scriptural association with the site, namely, Jesus' crown of thorns, the column of Jesus' scourging, and the stones of the martyrdom of Stephen.[36]

Looted and burned in 966, the Byzantine basilica (56 x 37 meters) lay in ruins when the Crusaders arrived; they restored it as one of the gemstones of Crusader Jerusalem. Built upon the same foundations, it was eleven meters longer to the west than the Byzantine church (67 x 37 meters). The current Cenacle, which occupies but a small area of the former churches, has been dated to the fourteenth century; it was more likely built in the late twelfth century before the Crusader church was destroyed (see station 6).

In the mid-thirteenth century, the church was dismantled by the Mamluks, who repurposed the stone. The Franciscans possessed the site from 1335 until they were expelled from the Cenacle in the 1520s upon orders of the Ottoman sultan Suleiman the Magnificent (d. 1566) when it was subsequently turned into a mosque. The large mihrab, which indicates the

---

34. Bordeaux Pilgrim, *Travels* 592; for the Epiphanius reference (*Treatise on Weights and Measures* 14), see Wilkinson, *Jerusalem Pilgrims*, 351.

35. On the Cenacle and the early Jerusalem church, see Murphy-O'Connor, "Cenacle."

36. See John 19:1–5 (the crown of thorns); Matt 27:26 (the scourging of Jesus); Acts 7:54–60 (the stoning of Stephen). The Gospel accounts do not refer to a column associated with Jesus' scourging.

direction of prayer toward Mecca, remains in place, and there are qur'anic inscriptions on the windows and walls. Since 1948, the surrounding area has become a Jewish Yeshiva with the Cenacle, a Status Quo site, under the administration of the Israeli Ministry of Interior.

Of the Christian sites of Jerusalem, Holy Sion is one of the hardest to envision; consequently, its historical importance for Christian pilgrimage and the Jerusalem church can be easy to underappreciate. While a number of modern shrines have been rebuilt upon their original Byzantine or Crusader foundations, the area of Holy Sion has been broken up and significantly reshaped. Besides the medieval Cenacle, there are some scant ruins in the basement of the Dormition Abbey. Moreover, while Holy Sion was a large rectangular basilica, today, the area is dominated by a massive circular church, the Dormition Abbey, dedicated in 1910.

Returning to the translation of Sion to the Western Hill, once the place-name moved, its associations eventually followed suit, influencing both Christian imagination and some actual commemorations. Although ancient Sion was on the Eastern Hill, for Byzantine Christians, the Western Hill (Mount Sion) was both the center of the New Testament church *and* the heart of Old Testament Jerusalem. This, no doubt, spurred supersessionist thinking—that the New Testament church had supplanted the Old Testament past, literally on the same hill. At the same time, Byzantine Christians brought the two together. *The Armenian Lectionary* lists a feast on December 25 at Holy Sion for "James and David"—that is, James the Just, the first bishop of Jerusalem, and King David.[37] This appears at first to be an odd combination of biblical figures until the pair is understood as the respective figureheads of New and Old Testament Sion (i.e., the Christian and Jewish founders of Jerusalem): it was the quintessential feast of Holy Sion. Similarly, the identification of Sion with the Western Hill eventually gave rise to David's tomb—originally a medieval Christian commemoration—located today underneath the Cenacle (cf. 1 Kgs 2:10).[38] Recognized by all three faiths, David's tomb was a primary reason why the Ottomans evicted the Franciscans from the site in the sixteenth century. After the War of 1948, when Jews lost access to the Western Wall in the Old City, the tomb of David became a focal point for Jewish devotion. The centuries-old

---

37. *Armenian Lectionary* 71; see Wilkinson, *Egeria's Travels*, 192.

38. See Limor, "Origins of a Tradition." The tomb of James, David's counterpart, is nearby in the Armenian Cathedral.

tradition of the so-called Tower of David inside Jaffa Gate likewise stems from the association of David with the Western Hill (Mount Sion).[39]

PILGRIMAGE TEXTS: HOLY SION

Theodosius, *Topography of the Holy Land* **7b (c. 518):** From Golgotha it is 200 paces to Holy Sion which is the Mother of All Churches: this Sion our Lord Christ founded with the apostles.

Commemoratorium 2 (c. 808): At Holy Sion 17 presbyters and clergy, not counting two who are dedicated to God as hermits.

---

39. On the discussion of Holy Sion, see Aist, *Christian Topography*, 135–47; Pringle, *Churches*, 261–87; Schick, *Christian Communities*, 335–36; Murphy-O'Connor, *Holy Land*, 115–18.

Station 6

The Cenacle

The Cenacle, a medieval structure that commemorates the Last Supper and Pentecost, is open daily from 8:00–18:00. It is closed on Yom Kippur. Admission is free. Free toilets are nearby.

COMMEMORATING STATION 6: THE CENACLE

Group readings are generally better outside but can be done inside the Cenacle.

- Begin in prayer.
- Review the background information for Holy Sion (above).
- Read the background information, pilgrimage texts, and Scripture readings for the Cenacle.
- What details emerge as you read the story of the Last Supper? How does Jesus washing the disciples' feet translate today?
- Find the reused Crusader capital of the pelican mother, which is an ancient eucharistic image. It is on top of a column supporting the Ottoman-era baldachin (small dome) over the stairs near the exit.
- Reflect on the Pentecost story: the descent of the Holy Spirit, the beginning of the church, and the multilingual (global, multicultural) nature of Christianity. How is Holy Land pilgrimage today a legacy of Pentecost?
- Note the presence of Arab-speaking Jews in the Pentecost story. There have been Arab-speaking Christians in the Holy Land for two

thousand years. Today, Palestinian Christians trace their identity to Pentecost. Pray for the indigenous Christians of the Holy Land.

- Note signs of the Cenacle's former use as a mosque during the Ottoman and British Mandate periods.
- Observe the bronze sculpture of the olive tree in the back of the room. A peace offering from Pope John Paul II, the three branches represent the Abrahamic faiths. Say a prayer of peace for the children of Abraham.
- Enjoy the views from the rooftop terrace.
- Make an optional visit to the tomb of David.

BACKGROUND INFORMATION: THE CENACLE

Beginning with the ground floor of the Cenacle (the tomb of David), the suggestion by Pinkerfeld that the building was a former Roman-period synagogue—largely on the belief that an apse was oriented toward the temple—has been more convincingly explained by Wilkinson as an exedra in the wall of the sacristy (diaconicon) of the Byzantine church.[40] While the walls of the room represent the oldest remains of Holy Sion, there are no identified ruins of a pre-Constantinian religious structure, whether Jewish or Christian, which doesn't dismiss the possibility that one existed.

According to Adomnán's drawing of Holy Sion (fig. 14), the Last Supper commemoration was located in the southeast corner of the basilica, which agrees with Epiphanius, who states that it was south of the altar. *The Armenian Guide* likewise places it on the south. Although the texts refer to the space as the Upper Room, it is unclear whether it was located on the ground floor or in an upper gallery (i.e., an actual upper room). While mentioning commemorations of the biblical Upper Room, *The Armenian Guide* explicitly states that there was no upper room in the church. The Byzantine basilica was looted and burned in 966.

The Crusaders rebuilt the church with the Last Supper commemoration (the Cenacle) in an upper gallery in the southeast corner of the basilica. The Cenacle spanned the width of the two southern aisles of the church with its northern wall adjoining the southern line of the nave. At

---

40. See Pringle, *Churches*, 272, which discusses the views of Pinkerfeld, "David's Tomb," and Wilkinson, *Jerusalem as Jesus Knew It*.

some point after the building of the Crusader church, the Cenacle was remodeled.

To spring ahead, the final demise of the Kingdom of Jerusalem took place in 1291 with the capture of Acre. Soon afterward in 1309, the Franciscans established a presence on Mount Sion, succeeding in the 1330s with the financial help of Robert of Anjou (d. 1343), king of Naples and titular king of Jerusalem, to purchase the Cenacle from the Mamluk sultan al-Nasir Muhammad (d. 1341). Two centuries later, on March 18, 1523, the Ottoman sultan Suleiman the Magnificent ordered his governor in Damascus to remove the Franciscans from Mount Sion. The directive was rescinded upon Venetian intervention but not before the friars had been expelled from the Cenacle. On June 2, 1551, they were completely banished from Mount Sion, relocating to the northwest corner of the city by the end of the decade where their headquarters remain today.

So, when was the Cenacle built? The most cited opinion, based upon the view of Eugene-Melchior de Vogüé (d. 1910), was that the work was done by architects from Cyprus in the mid-fourteenth century after the Franciscans purchased the site in the 1330s. It has since been noted that the style was already outdated in the fourteenth century, while, architecturally, studies of the building indicate that the Cenacle was remodeled while the southern walls of the nave were still standing. Since the Crusader basilica was otherwise destroyed soon after 1187, this points to an earlier date. An examination of the building in 1981–82 convincingly argued that the work was completed in the late twelfth century, or in the final years of the original Kingdom of Jerusalem (1099–1187). Although the style is advanced for its time, its features appear in French and English buildings of the 1170s–80s.[41]

Today, the Cenacle commemorates both Pentecost and the Last Supper. The languages of visiting pilgrims evoke the setting of Pentecost; on the other hand, the Cenacle is not a place where Christians can celebrate Eucharist (the Last Supper), which is one of the historical ironies of Christian Jerusalem. Religious ceremonies are not allowed; however, the following exceptions are protected by the Status Quo: the feast of Pentecost according to the Catholic, Orthodox, and Armenian rites, Holy Thursday for the Franciscans, and an ecumenical service on the last Thursday in January for the Week of Prayer for Christian Unity.

41. For a detailed discussion of the Cenacle, see Pringle, *Churches*, 261–87, esp. 272, 285. On reasons why the Cenacle may have been spared when the Crusader basilica was destroyed, which includes its association with the tomb of David, see Pringle, *Churches*, 268.

The Stations

Inside, a bronze sculpture of an olive tree stands against the northern wall. A gift of Pope John Paul II (d. 2005), the tree and its three branches symbolize the Abrahamic faiths—Judaism, Christianity, and Islam. Around the base of the tree is a stalk of wheat and a vine representing the bread and wine of the Last Supper. The other eucharistic symbol in the room is a reused Crusader capital depicting a mother pelican allowing her young to drink blood from her chest. According to an ancient legend that precedes Christianity, in time of need the mother pelican wounds herself in the breast, feeding her young with her blood to prevent their starvation even to the point of losing her life. Early Christianity adopted the symbol as a eucharistic image of Jesus' sacrificial death.

Leave the Cenacle through the exit door near the pelican capital, and ascend to the rooftop terrace accessed by three flights of wooden stairs. To the north are views of Benedictine, Franciscan, and Armenian monasteries, a visual reminder of the historical Christian connection with Mount Sion. To the east is a panoramic view of the Mount of Olives. In the northwest corner of the terrace is a small building known as the President's Room. After the War of 1948 when Jerusalem was under Jordanian rule and Jews were barred from the Old City, the summit of Mount Sion was among the closest places that Jews could get to the Western Wall. On holy days, Yitzhak Ben-Zvi (d. 1963), Israel's second president, hosted Jewish guests on the terrace, reading Torah as they looked over the city.

PILGRIMAGE TEXTS: THE CENACLE

***Breviarius* e (c. 400):** You go on from there to the basilica containing the column at which the Lord Jesus was struck. There is a mark where he held onto it. From that you go to the sacrarium. It contains the Stone with which St. Stephen was stoned. In the centre of the basilica is the crown of thorns which they gave the Lord. There too is the Upper Room where the Lord taught his disciples when he had the supper.

The Piacenza Pilgrim, *Travels* 22 (c. 570): From there, we came to the basilica of Holy Sion, where there are many marvelous things, among which is the cornerstone rejected by the builders that is read about in the Bible. The Lord Jesus entered into this church, which was the house of Saint James, and he found this deformed stone lying in the middle: he picked it up and placed it in the corner. When you pick it up and hold it in your hands—and stand in the same corner listening—it sounds like the murmuring of a multitude of people. In the same church is the column where the Lord was scourged. On the column is such a mark: when he clung to the column, his chest stuck to the marble, and both of his hands—his fingers and palms—appear in the rock. The mark is so distinct that measurements can be taken from it: they wear them around their necks for ailments of every kind, and they are healed. On the same column is the horn from which David and the kings were anointed. Also in that church is the crown of thorns with which the Lord was crowned, and the lance with which the Lord was pierced in the side. And there are many rocks with which Stephen was stoned. There is also a small column where the cross of Blessed Peter has been placed, on which he was crucified in Rome. There too is the chalice of the apostles with which they celebrated Mass after the Lord's resurrection. And many other marvelous things which I cannot recall.

Sophronius, *Anacreontica* 20.55–72 (before 614): And, speeding on, may I pass to Sion where, in the likeness of fiery tongues, the Grace of God descended; where, when he had completed the mystic supper, the King of All teaching in humility washed his disciples' feet. Blessing of salvation, like rivers pour from that Rock where Mary handmaid of God . . . was laid out in death. Hail, Sion, radiant Sun of the universe! Night and day I long and yearn for thee. There, after shattering hell, and liberating the dead, the King of All, the Shatterer appeared there, the Friend.

Epiphanius, *Holy City* 7 (before 692): And to the right of the Pavement is Holy Sion, the House of God. And at the great door on the left is the place where the holy Apostles carried the body of the most holy Mother of God after her departure. And at the right part of the same door is the vent-hole of the Gehenna of Fire, and near it is set up the stone at which they scourged Christ our God. . . . To the right side of the altar is the Upper Room, where Christ had the Supper with his Disciples.

Bernard, *Journey to the Holy Places* 12 (870): In this city there is another church to the south, on Mount Sion . . . where the Lord washed the feet of his disciples, and the Lord's crown of thorns hangs there. This is the church where we are told Saint Mary died.

The Stations

SCRIPTURE READINGS: THE CENACLE

Matthew 26:17–30 (The Last Supper): On the first day of Unleavened Bread the disciples came to Jesus, saying, "Where do you want us to make the preparations for you to eat the Passover?" He said, "Go into the city to a certain man, and say to him, 'The Teacher says, My time is near; I will keep the Passover at your house with my disciples.'" So the disciples did as Jesus had directed them, and they prepared the Passover meal. When it was evening, he took his place with the twelve; and while they were eating, he said, "Truly I tell you, one of you will betray me." And they became greatly distressed and began to say to him one after another, "Surely not I, Lord?" He answered, "The one who has dipped his hand into the bowl with me will betray me. The Son of Man goes as it is written of him, but woe to that one by whom the Son of Man is betrayed! It would have been better for that one not to have been born." Judas, who betrayed him, said, "Surely not I, Rabbi?" He replied, "You have said so." While they were eating, Jesus took a loaf of bread, and after blessing it he broke it, gave it to the disciples, and said, "Take, eat; this is my body." Then he took a cup, and after giving thanks he gave it to them, saying, "Drink from it, all of you; for this is my blood of the covenant, which is poured out for many for the forgiveness of sins. I tell you, I will never again drink of this fruit of the vine until that day when I drink it new with you in my Father's kingdom." When they had sung the hymn, they went out to the Mount of Olives.

Luke 22:31–34 (Jesus predicts Peter's denial): "Simon, Simon, listen! Satan has demanded to sift all of you like wheat, but I have prayed for you that your own faith may not fail; and you, when once you have turned back, strengthen your brothers." And he said to him, "Lord, I am ready to go with you to prison and to death!" Jesus said, "I tell you, Peter, the cock will not crow this day, until you have denied three times that you know me."

John 13:1–16 (Jesus washes the disciples' feet): Now before the festival of the Passover, Jesus knew that his hour had come to depart from this world and go to the Father. Having loved his own who were in the world, he loved them to the end. The devil had already put it into the heart of Judas son of Simon Iscariot to betray him. And during supper Jesus, knowing that the Father had given all things into his hands, and that he had come from God and was going to God, got up from the table, took off his outer robe, and tied a towel around himself. Then he poured water into a basin and began to wash the disciples' feet and to wipe them with the towel that was tied around him. He came to Simon Peter, who said to him, "Lord, are you going to wash my feet?" Jesus answered, "You do not know now what I am doing, but later you will understand." Peter said to him, "You will never wash my feet." Jesus answered, "Unless I wash you, you have no share with me." Simon Peter said to him, "Lord, not my feet only but also my hands and my head!" Jesus said to him, "One who has bathed does not need to wash, except for the feet, but is entirely clean. And you are clean, though not all of you." For he knew who was to betray him; for this reason he said, "Not all of you are clean." After he had washed their feet, had put on his robe, and had returned to the table, he said to them, "Do you know what I have done to you? You call me Teacher and Lord—and you are right, for that is what I am. So if I, your Lord and Teacher, have washed your feet, you also ought to wash one another's feet. For I have set you an example, that you also should do as I have done to you."

Acts 2:1–11 (Pentecost): When the day of Pentecost had come, they were all together in one place. And suddenly from heaven there came a sound like the rush of a violent wind, and it filled the entire house where they were sitting. Divided tongues, as of fire, appeared among them, and a tongue rested on each of them. All of them were filled with the Holy Spirit and began to speak in other languages, as the Spirit gave them ability.

Now there were devout Jews from every nation under heaven living in Jerusalem. And at this sound the crowd gathered and was bewildered, because each one heard them speaking in the native language of each. Amazed and astonished, they asked, "Are not all these who are speaking Galileans? And how is it that we hear, each of us, in our own native language? Parthians, Medes, Elamites, and residents of Mesopotamia, Judea and Cappadocia, Pontus and Asia, Phrygia and Pamphylia, Egypt and the parts of Libya belonging to Cyrene, and visitors from Rome, both Jews and proselytes, Cretans and Arabs—in our own languages we hear them speaking about God's deeds of power."

Station 7
The Dormition Abbey

The Dormition Abbey, dedicated to Mary's "falling asleep" in death, is open Monday through Saturday from 9:00–17:00 and Sundays from 12:30–17:00. Admission is free. It has a gift shop, cafeteria, and toilets. There is a helpful English brochure. Also see http://www.dormitio.net/.

Fig. 15. Willibald of Eichstätt, c. 1950. Mosaic in the Basilica of the Dormition Abbey, Jerusalem. Photo by Cole Yeoman. Used with permission.

COMMEMORATING STATION 7: THE DORMITION ABBEY

Group readings and prayers can be done in the front courtyard of the Dormition Abbey; it may also be possible to use the basilica or the crypt of the church.

- Read the background information and pilgrimage texts for the Dormition Abbey.
- As you explore the church, be attentive to Old Testament images.
- Observe the images of Mary throughout the church.
- Find the mosaic of Willibald in the middle side altar on the right.
- Examine the creation-themed floor mosaic.
- Explore the crypt, which features an effigy of Mary.
- At the eastern end of the crypt, view the image of Pentecost with Mary in the midst.
- Visit the sparse archaeological ruins from the Byzantine and Crusader churches in the basement. The stairwell is between the gift shop and the cafeteria. On the wall is a reconstructed plan of the churches that is helpful for understanding the extent of the site and its relationship to the Cenacle.
- Have a drink in the cafeteria; spend time in the gift shop.
- End in prayer.

BACKGROUND INFORMATION: THE DORMITION ABBEY

The Dormition Tradition

Clarifying terms related to the end of Mary's life, the word *dormition* ("the falling asleep") has two connotations. It is used to refer to the type of death Mary experienced: one without suffering and sorrow. It can also indicate that she underwent something different from an earthly death. Although Mariology, at times, has been somewhat equivocal, the ancient sources clearly state that she died. According to tradition, at the end of her life, Mary's soul was received into heaven. Her body was subsequently entombed before being physically assumed into heaven where it was reunited with her soul. All stories regarding the end of Mary's life can be referred to as dormition traditions. Some but not all of the earliest sources include her assumption, thus, one can speak in terms of assumptionist and assumptionless texts.[42]

Summarizing the Jerusalem tradition: Mary lived on Mount Sion serving the Jerusalem church. Before she dies, the apostles, who were already dispersed in mission, are miraculously transported back to Jerusalem to be at her side. After her death, the apostles take Mary in procession to Gethsemane. On the way, a Jew named Jephonias tries to seize her body, but his attempt is thwarted by an angel of the Lord (see station 11). The funeral procession continues to Gethsemane, where Mary is entombed. Three days later, Mary's body is taken into heaven, leaving an empty tomb (see station 12).

In the pre-Crusader period, two separate churches and one monument commemorated the story: Holy Sion (the place of her death), the Jephonias monument (the funeral incident), and the Church of Mary's Tomb (the place of her entombment and assumption). They were *complementary sites*, remembering separate events of the same story, not competing sites of different communities.

As opposed to traditions of Mary's birth that appear as early as the late second century, stories about the end of Mary's life are much later. While strands were circulating in the fourth century, a recognized tradition emerges no earlier than the fifth century. Thus, the dormition tradition postdates the founding of Holy Sion. Although the commemoration became one of the three primary memories of the church, it is later than Pentecost and the Last Supper.

Still, the Jerusalem tradition is earlier and more dominant than that of Ephesus, which only appears in the ninth century. Mary's association with Ephesus was bolstered in the late nineteenth century when her house was "discovered" based upon visions by Anne Catherine Emmerich (d. 1824), an Augustinian nun living in Germany.

Traditional motifs of the dormition icon depict Mary prone on her death bed with the apostles gathered around her, sometimes literally on the clouds that conveyed them to Jerusalem. The resurrected Jesus stands behind Mary in the center of the image holding a small infant that represents

---

42. See Shoemaker, *Ancient Traditions*.

Jesus receiving her soul into heaven. Eastern Orthodox icons commonly show the incident between the angel and Jephonias in the foreground.

Although Mary's assumption has been part of church tradition for centuries, it was first proclaimed as a dogma by Pope Pius XII on November 1, 1950 (*Munificentissimus Deus*). The explanation given for Mary's bodily assumption, as opposed to other saints who have not been assumed, is linked to the previous dogma of the Immaculate Conception (1854). The 1950 declaration states: "According to the general rule, God does not will to grant to the just the full effect of the victory over death until the end of time has come. And so it is that the bodies of even the just are corrupted after death, and only on the last day will they be joined, each to its own glorious soul." It was different for Mary, who "completely overcame sin by her Immaculate Conception, and as a result she was not subject to the law of remaining in the corruption of the grave, and she did not have to wait until the end of time for the redemption of her body."[43]

It's worth noting that the Jerusalem Circuit incorporated the route of Mary's funeral. Similarly, the Crusaders celebrated the feast of the Assumption with a procession from Holy Sion to the Church of Mary's Tomb, while today the Greeks mark the feast on August 25 by processing Mary's effigy from the Holy Sepulchre to her tomb where it is venerated until September 5.

The Dormition Abbey

On the same day, October 31, 1898, that Kaiser Wilhelm II dedicated the Lutheran Church of the Redeemer in the Old City, he purchased the grounds of the Dormition Abbey from the Ottoman sultan, Abdul Hamid II, on behalf of German Catholic interests, promptly handing it over to the *Deutschen Vereins vom Heiligen Lande*, the German Catholic association of the Holy Land, to construct a church. The kaiser, who saw himself as emperor of both Protestants and Catholics, remained the legal owner of the land until 1924 when it was transferred to the archbishop of Cologne.

Designed by the Cologne diocesan architect, Heinrich Renard, construction of the Dormition Abbey began in 1900; it was consecrated in 1910. Dominating Jerusalem's Western Hill, the church is modeled upon St. Gereon's Basilica, a Romanesque church in Cologne. It also resembles Charlemagne's Palatine Chapel in Aachen consecrated in 805: built at a

---

43. See https://www.vatican.va/content/pius-xii/en/apost_constitutions/documents/hf_p-xii_apc_19501101_munificentissimus-deus.html.

The Stations

time when foreign powers, particularly Britain, France, Russia, and Germany, were positioning themselves in Jerusalem during the late Ottoman period, the church evokes the imperial legacy of Germany's past.

Although the full plan of the church has never been realized (e.g., it was intended to have interior marble), there is a wealth of artistic decorations inside. The large apse mosaic of Mary and child, designed in 1939 by Radbrod Commandeur (d. 1955), dominates the sanctuary. Jesus holds a book with words from John 12:46: "I am the light of the world." Under the image, Isa 7:14, written in Latin, conveys the theme of the apse: "A virgin shall conceive and give birth to a son and will call him Emmanuel." Below the verse are paired images of eight prophets who foretold the birth of the Messiah (from left to right): Micah, Isaiah, Jeremiah, Ezekiel, Daniel, Haggai, Zechariah, and Malachi.

From back to front, the side altars on the left are dedicated to St. Boniface, St. John the Baptist, and St. Joseph; on the right, to St. Benedict, St. Willibald, and the Magi. Our attention is captured by the mosaic behind the Willibald altar, which depicts Willibald along with early church leaders of Bavaria paying homage to Mary, the region's patron saint. We are walking, of course, in Willibald's footsteps, one of the central protagonists of the Jerusalem Circuit. His image in the German Benedictine Dormition Abbey is particularly fitting: not only did he visit Holy Sion as a Jerusalem pilgrim, he was a Benedictine monk from Anglo-Saxon England who served as the bishop of Eichstätt, Germany, for nearly forty-five years (see fig. 15).

The round floor mosaic, designed by Mauritius Gisler, a former monk of the abbey, celebrates the created world. Executed in 1932, the mosaic was inspired by the recently discovered Byzantine synagogue at Beit Alpha uncovered in 1928, in particular its use of the zodiac. In the middle of the mosaic, three intertwined rings of the Trinity accompanied by the thrice-written *agios* ("holy, holy, holy") mark the center of creation. Moving outward, the Trinity reveals itself to the major and minor prophets. The wide middle band is devoted to the four evangelists and the twelve apostles who carried the light of God out into the world, represented by the months and signs of the zodiac. Forming the boundaries of creation, the outer circle contains the words of Prov 8:23–25: "Ages ago I was set up, at the first, before the beginning of the earth. When there were no depths I was brought forth, where there were no spring abounding with water. Before the mountains had been shaped, before the hills, I was bought forth."

At the back left of the sanctuary, a stone circular staircase leads to the crypt. Created by Radbrod Commandeur in 1937, the focal point of the crypt is an effigy of Mary on her death bed under a circular ciborium marking the traditional location of her death.[44] Her hands and face are made of ivory; her robe was originally silver and gold. Above her in the inner dome of the ciborium, Mary is accompanied by six biblical women—Eve, Miriam, Ruth, Esther, Jael, and Judith—in contrast to the male apostles who gather around her in the dormition story. Circling the portrait of Jesus in the center is a line from Song 2:10: "Arise, my love, my fair one, and come away."

Damaged by shelling during the War of 1948, the Dormition Abbey was occupied by the Israeli military from 1948–51. After the war, only the wooden core of Mary's statue remained. The ivory of her hands and face have been repaired; the silver and gold have not been replaced. According to the abbey's website: "The wars of human beings and their violence toward one another leave their traces also in the faces of the saints. Yet the wounds and needs of human beings have their place with the saints."[45]

The adjacent niche at the western end of the crypt depicts Mary's dormition. The altar table is supported by a section of a column from the Byzantine church; the mosaic lettering on the middle ring bears the famous title of Holy Sion: *mater omnium ecclesiarum* ("the mother of all churches"). At the eastern end of the crypt is the Pentecost altar, also executed by Radbrod Commandeur.

Outside, the abbey's bell tower has both Western Christian and Islamic features. Surmounted by a cross (as well as a rooster), the tower was respectfully placed where its shadow would never fall upon what at the time was an adjacent mosque—none other than the Cenacle! Finally, based upon a Christian inscription discovered in the Sinai in the 1970s, the symbol of the Benedictine community of the Dormition Abbey is the rainbow cross.[46]

---

44. The consistent testimony of Crusader texts as well as Adomnán's drawing of Holy Sion locates Mary's death in the northwest corner of the Byzantine-Crusader basilica. The location of Mary's effigy is in general accord with the traditional location of her death.

45. See http://www.dormitio.net/english/en.places/en.abbey.church/index.html.

46. See http://www.dormitio.net/english/en.community/en.roots/en.rainbow.cross/index.html.

The Stations

PILGRIMAGE TEXTS: THE DORMITION ABBEY

Sophronius, *Anacreontica* **20.55, 64–66 (c. 614):** And, speeding on, may I pass to Sion ... where Mary handmaid of God ... was laid out in death.

Epiphanius, *Holy Place* **7 (before 692):** And to the right of the Pavement is Holy Sion, the House of God. And at the great door on the left is the place where the holy Apostles carried the body of the most holy Mother of God after her departure.

Hugeburc (Willibald), *Life of Willibald* **19–20 (724–26):** [Willibald] got up, and went off to visit the church called Holy Sion, which stands in the middle of Jerusalem. ... St. Mary departed this life right in the middle of Jerusalem at the place called Holy Sion.

Bernard, *Journey to the Holy Places* **12 (870):** In this city there is another church to the south, on Mount Sion. ... This is the church where we are told Saint Mary died.

Station 8
The Church of Holy Wisdom: Jesus' Trial Before Pilate

Fig. 16. *Christ's Scourging at the Pillar*, c. 1400. Styria, Austria. Diptych with the Passion of Christ. Tempera and gold on wood oak. The Cleveland Museum of Art. Public domain.

The Stations

DIRECTIONS:
HOLY SION TO HOLY WISDOM

From Holy Sion, pilgrims of the late Byzantine period descended the Western Hill until they reached the eastern cardo. Turning north, they took the cardo to Holy Wisdom, which was west of the Temple Mount. Tracing the route today: upon leaving the area of Holy Sion, return to Sion Gate, turning right at the city wall immediately before the gate. Keeping the wall on your left, walk along the stepped sidewalk that runs against and parallel to the wall as it descends the Western Hill. The pathway is marked by pedestrian signs: follow directions to the Tanners' Gate. As you continue down the hill with the wall on the left, the tarmac road (Ma'ale HaShalom) will appear on the right, parallel to the sidewalk. After the second bus shelter, take the path that veers off to the left which turns into a boardwalk: keep following the signs for the Tanners' Gate. As you enter through the small opening of the Tanners' Gate—and back inside the city—you are on the southern end of the eastern cardo: note the painted mural of the cardo directly in front of you. Turn immediately to the right, proceeding to the tarmac road that allows motorized traffic through the Dung Gate. Carefully cross the road, turning left on the sidewalk that leads to the Western Wall Plaza. Go through security and enter the plaza.

THE STATION

During the Byzantine period, the Church of Holy Wisdom (Hagia Sophia) was dedicated to Jesus' trial before Pilate. The church was destroyed in the Persian conquest of 614, and while its specific location has not been identified, we know from textual sources that it was somewhere west of the western wall of the Temple Mount. The Western Wall Plaza is a suitable location to commemorate the station. Situated in the Central Valley, the plaza offers instructive views of the topography of Jerusalem: looking north, to the right is the former Temple Mount (the Eastern Hill); to the left is the Upper City (the Western Hill).

COMMEMORATING STATION 8: HOLY WISDOM

In the Western Wall Plaza:

- Begin in prayer.
- Read the background information, pilgrimage texts, and Scripture readings for Holy Wisdom.
- What images stand out regarding Jesus' trial before Pilate? What details emerge from the Scripture readings?
- What strikes you about the account of the Piacenza Pilgrim?
- What is it like to commemorate a site that no longer exists?
- Observe the historical and religious contrasts that mark the area around you.[47]
- Spend additional time in the plaza.
- End in prayer.

BACKGROUND INFORMATION: HOLY WISDOM

During the Byzantine period, there was a church specifically dedicated to Jesus' trial before Pilate, with pilgrim texts describing the praetorium (John 18:28) and the stone upon which Jesus was scourged (John 19:1). Holy Wisdom was destroyed in the Persian conquest of 614 and was not rebuilt. Although ruins of the church have never been found, from textual descriptions and the Madaba Map, we know that the church was west of the Temple Mount on or near the lower section of the eastern cardo. This corresponds to the area near today's Western Wall Plaza, perhaps slightly to the northwest.

After the destruction of Holy Wisdom, Jesus' trial before Pilate was transferred to Mount Sion not far from the pre-Crusader location of Caiaphas's house, the setting of Jesus' trial before the chief priests and Peter's denial of Jesus. The Pilate commemoration moved again in the late Crusader period to the former Antonia Fortress at the northwest corner of the Temple Mount, which consequently became the first station of the Via Dolorosa.[48] The belief that Pilate took residence at the Antonia Fortress when he came to Jerusalem for the Passover feast was encouraged in modern times by the misidentification of some suggestive ruins, namely, the Ecce

---

47. On the history of the Western Wall Plaza, see Lemire, *In the Shadow*, and Cohen-Hattab, "Struggles."

48. See Murphy-O'Connor, "Tracing the Via Dolorosa."

Homo arch and the Lithostrotos in the basement of the Ecce Homo Guesthouse. They have subsequently been dated to the Hadrian period in the second century. Scholars now generally accept that Pilate spent Passover in Herod the Great's former palace near Jaffa Gate.

PILGRIMAGE TEXTS: HOLY WISDOM

The Bordeaux Pilgrim, *Travels* 593 (333): As you leave there and pass through the wall of Sion towards the Gate of Neapolis [walking north on the *western* cardo], down in the valley on your right you have some walls where Pilate had his house, the Praetorium where the Lord's case was heard before he suffered.

Theodosius, *Topography* 7b (c. 518): From Holy Sion to the House of Caiaphas, which is now the Church of Saint Peter, it is about 50 paces. From the House of Caiaphas to the Praetorium of Pilate it is about 100 paces: the Church of Saint Sophia is there.

***Breviarius* A, 5 (c. 525):** From there you go to the house of Pilate, where he had the Lord scourged and handed him over to the Jews. There is a large basilica there, and in it the chamber where they stripped him and he was scourged. It is called Holy Wisdom.

The Piacenza Pilgrim, *Travels* 23 (c. 570): We prayed at the praetorium, where the Lord was tried, now the basilica of Saint Sophia, which is in front of the ruins of Solomon's temple, by the portico of Solomon, along the street that runs to spring of Siloam. In that basilica is the seat where Pilate sat when he tried the Lord. There is a rectangular stone that stood in the middle of the praetorium, on which the person being tried was elevated, so he could be heard and seen by all the people. The Lord stood on that stone when he was tried by Pilate, and even now his footprints remain there. He had a small, delicate, and handsome foot. As depicted in an image placed in the praetorium that was painted while he was living, he was of common height with a handsome appearance, curly hair, and a well-formed hand with long fingers. From this stone where he stood, many wonders occur: taking measurements of his footprints, people wear them for various ailments, and they are healed. The rock is decorated with silver and gold.

Sophronius, *Anacreontica* 20.73–80 (before 614): Then let me leave Sion's summit and, embracing the stone where for me my creator was smitten go down to the House and the Stone; [and] let me fall to the ground and venerate—I am oppressed by tears!—the spot where the foremost of those who love Wisdom heard his own sentence.

PILGRIMAGE TEXTS (AFTER 614): JESUS BEFORE PILATE ON MOUNT SION

The Armenian Guide 5 (c. 630): And on the right of Holy Sion stands the Palace of Pilate called Gabbatha, containing the stone on which the Saviour stood before Pilate, and upon which his footprints are to be seen to this day.

Epiphanius, *Holy City* 7–8 (before 692): And to the right of the Pavement is Holy Sion, the House of God. And at the great door on the left is the place where the holy Apostles carried the body of the most holy Mother of God after her departure. And at the right part of the same door is the vent-hole of the Gehenna of Fire, and near it is set up the stone at which they scourged Christ our God. And at the holy doors of the sanctuary are the footprints of Christ. There he stood when he was judged by Pilate. To the right side of the altar is the Upper Room, where Christ had the Supper with his Disciples. . . . And in the apse of Holy Sion (or rather of the Praetorium) there is a small structure with four columns containing the coal-brazier. In this place Saint Peter was asked the question by the little maid. And he denied Christ three times, and straightway the cock crowed. And in the same place is the palace of Pilate, and also of Annas and Caiaphas and of Caesar. Outside the city on the right, near the wall, is a church to which Peter went out and wept bitterly.

SCRIPTURE READINGS: HOLY WISDOM

John 18:28–40 (Jesus before Pilate): Then they took Jesus from Caiaphas to Pilate's headquarters. It was early in the morning. They themselves did not enter the headquarters, so as to avoid ritual defilement and to be able to eat the Passover. So Pilate went out to them and said, "What accusation do you bring against this man?" They answered, "If this man were not a criminal, we would not have handed him over to you." Pilate said to them, "Take him yourselves and judge him according to your law." The Jews replied, "We are not permitted to put anyone to death." (This was to fulfill what Jesus had said when he indicated the kind of death he was to die.) Then Pilate entered the headquarters again, summoned Jesus, and asked him, "Are you the King of the Jews?" Jesus answered, "Do you ask this on your own, or did others tell you about me?" Pilate replied, "I am not a Jew, am I? Your own nation and the chief priests have handed you over to me. What have you done?" Jesus answered, "My kingdom is not from this world. If my kingdom were from this world, my followers would be fighting to keep me from being handed over to the Jews. But as it is, my kingdom is not from here." Pilate asked him, "So you are a king?" Jesus answered, "You say that I am a king. For this I was born, and for this I came into the world, to testify to the truth. Everyone who belongs to the truth listens to my voice." Pilate asked him, "What is truth?" After he had said this, he went out to the Jews again and told them, "I find no case against him. But you have a custom that I release someone for you at the Passover. Do you want me to release for you the King of the Jews?" They shouted in reply, "Not this man, but Barabbas!" Now Barabbas was a bandit.

John 19:1-16 (Jesus is sentenced to death): Then Pilate took Jesus and had him flogged. And the soldiers wove a crown of thorns and put it on his head, and they dressed him in a purple robe. They kept coming up to him, saying, "Hail, King of the Jews!" and striking him on the face. Pilate went out again and said to them, "Look, I am bringing him out to you to let you know that I find no case against him." So Jesus came out, wearing the crown of thorns and the purple robe. Pilate said to them, "Here is the man!" When the chief priests and the police saw him, they shouted, "Crucify him! Crucify him!" Pilate said to them, "Take him yourselves and crucify him; I find no case against him." The Jews answered him, "We have a law, and according to that law he ought to die because he has claimed to be the Son of God." Now when Pilate heard this, he was more afraid than ever. He entered his headquarters again and asked Jesus, "Where are you from?" But Jesus gave him no answer. Pilate therefore said to him, "Do you refuse to speak to me? Do you not know that I have power to release you, and power to crucify you?" Jesus answered him, "You would have no power over me unless it had been given you from above; therefore the one who handed me over to you is guilty of a greater sin." From then on Pilate tried to release him, but the Jews cried out, "If you release this man, you are no friend of the emperor. Everyone who claims to be a king sets himself against the emperor." When Pilate heard these words, he brought Jesus outside and sat on the judge's bench at a place called The Stone Pavement, or in Hebrew Gabbatha. Now it was the day of Preparation for the Passover; and it was about noon. He said to the Jews, "Here is your King!" They cried out, "Away with him! Away with him! Crucify him!" Pilate asked them, "Shall I crucify your King?" The chief priests answered, "We have no king but the emperor." Then he handed him over to them to be crucified.

Stations 9–10
The Church of St. Anne

DIRECTIONS: HOLY WISDOM TO ST. ANNE'S

Keeping the Western Wall on your right as you leave the plaza, take the street through the archway to the left of the toilets, and continue for appropriately five hundred meters. You are walking north up the Central Valley on el-Wad Street (the Valley Street) following the general route of the eastern cardo. Turn right on the Via Dolorosa, which is the first street on the right for motorized traffic after leaving the Western Wall Plaza. Continue east on the Via Dolorosa for four hundred meters until you reach the Church of St. Anne on the left, a block before Lion's Gate.

THE STATIONS AT ST. ANNE'S

The site of St. Anne's has historically contained two commemorations: Jesus' healing of the paralytic in John 5 and the nativity of Mary, now respectively the archaeological ruins of the pool of Bethesda (station 9) and the adjacent twelfth-century Church of St. Anne (station 10). A Byzantine church built upon the Bethesda pools commemorated both events. Stations 9 and 10 can be done in either order.

    The White Fathers (French: *Pères Blancs*), officially known as the Missionaries of Africa (Latin: *Missionarii Africae*), are the spiritual custodians of the site. Founded in Algeria in 1868, they are a missionary community of priests and brothers working primarily in Africa and with Africans. The

St. Anne's community includes priests and candidates preparing for the missionary priesthood, the latter pursuing their theological studies at the Salesian Theological Institute in Jerusalem. Twice a year, they hold three-month biblical and spiritual sessions in French and English, primarily for African missionaries but open to others. St. Anne's is the property of France, with the White Fathers owning areas around the edge of the site.

Admission to St. Anne's is 12 NIS. Students are 10 NIS. The site is open Monday through Saturday from 8:00–12:00 and 14:00–17:00. It is closed on Sundays. There are toilets on the site. See https://ste-anne-jerusalem.org/en/.

Station 9
The Pool of Bethesda

COMMEMORATING STATION 9: THE POOL OF BETHESDA

In or near the archaeological ruins:

- Begin in prayer.
- Read the background information, pilgrimage texts, and Scripture readings for the pool of Bethesda.
- Read the informational boards overlooking the site. The biblical site of Bethesda consisted of two deep pools separated by a dike.
- Observe the grounds, stones, light, and shadows. What initial impressions do you have of the place?
- Concentrate for a while on the southern pool, which like the northern pool is only partially excavated. From the dike in the middle of the ruins, the area of the southern pool extends to the south under the lot opposite the entrance to the church. Find the stairwell that marks the southeastern corner of the southern pool (between the entrance to the site and the church).
- Walk through the excavations to the west end of the southern pool. Looking down at the floor of the basin, observe the stepped landing leading into the pool which alternates between short and long steps. The landing provided controlled access to the pool, allowing people to stand, sit, or recline at various levels.

- Locate the dike separating the pools. A sluice at the base of the dike allowed water to be moved from the northern to the southern pool, providing one explanation for the stirring of the waters described in John 5:4–7.
- The western end of the Byzantine church extended onto the dike; its supporting buttresses were literally immersed into the waters of the pool. What does being where it happened do to our experience of the story? What is it like to be immersed in a biblical story—physically, spiritually, emotionally?
- Observe the remnants of the shallow pools at the eastern end of the archaeological site. The pools were a part of a Late Roman cult to Asclepius, the god of medicine and healing: the site continued to be associated with miracles, cures, and healings after the time of Jesus. Reflect upon the continuity of holy sites and places of healing.
- Reread John 5 as you scan the ruined pools. What details emerge from the Scripture? What stories are told by the site?
- Take photos; sit and reflect.
- End in prayer.

BACKGROUND INFORMATION: THE POOL OF BETHESDA

The pool of Bethesda (also the Sheep Pool, or the Probatica) was outside the walls of Jerusalem at the time of Jesus. The Sheep Gate mentioned in John 5:2 presumably refers to an access point to the Temple Mount nearby to the south (see Neh 3:1; 12:39). The description of the pool as having five porticos is an enigmatic reference to a double pool, which is mentioned in the Copper Scroll of the Dead Sea Scrolls and clarified by Origen in the mid-third century: four porticos "were found around the edges and another across the middle."[49]

The site consisted of two adjacent pools, more or less rectangular (trapezoidal), separated by a 6.5-meter-wide dike (also referred to as a dam, causeway, and partition wall). While the basins have been partially

---

49. Origen, *Commentary on St. John* 5.2.

The Stations

excavated, no archaeology from the superstructure of the biblical site, including the porticos, has been identified.

The northern pool (53 m x 40 m) collected rainwater off the Bethesda (*Bethzatha, Bethsaida*) hill during the winter months of the rainy season. A rock-cut sluice allowed the northern reservoir to replenish the southern pool (52 m x 47 m) with collected rain water creating the necessary conditions for a large public mikveh, which was located near the northern entrance to the temple precincts. The movement of water produced by the opening of the sluice provides a possible explanation of the stirring of the waters mentioned in John 5:4–7. The pools were deep (13.5 m), making it difficult to envision physically disabled people lying along the water's edge as described in John 5. However, partial excavations of the southern pool have revealed a series of descending landings along the pool's western end that could have facilitated a controlled approach to the water and provided space to recline.

Immediately to the east of the twinned pools—in the area that was subsequently covered by the eastern end of the Byzantine basilica—are some shallow pools. Excavations have found votive offerings of the cult of Asclepius, the Roman god of medicine, as well as signs of a pagan temple that date to the Late Roman period. Used by both Jews and Gentiles, the Bethesda site remained a place of healing after the time of Jesus.

The Church of the Paralytic (45 m x 18 m), also known as the Basilica of St. Mary, was built by the mid-fifth century. The eastern half of the basilica covered the shallow pools, while its western end rested on the dike: its supporting buttresses extended down into the pools some thirteen meters (forty-three feet) below the church. Epitomizing the religious imagination of the Byzantine period, the location and structure of the church immersed pilgrims into the narrative setting of the paralytic healing. The church was damaged in 614 but continued in use for most of the Early Islamic period. It was destroyed at some point before the arrival of the Crusaders, who built a small chapel on the dike—upon the ruins of the Byzantine church.

Early on, the Byzantine sources indicate that the pools were suffering from siltation, and in the Crusader period, an alternative site, the pool of Israel located against the northern wall of the temple precincts, emerged a stone's throw to the south. For a while, the commemoration was remembered at both places. Crusader pilgrimage texts mention the legend that the wood of Jesus' cross, rejected for use in Solomon's temple, had been thrown into the pool of Bethesda where it remained for centuries. According to the *Second Guide*, "Near [the Church of Saint Anne] is the Sheep Pool which had five porches. The Pool is the place where those who visit are told that the Wood of the Cross remained for a long time, but the Templers show you another Pool and say that that is the Sheep Pool."[50] Eventually, the commemoration become exclusively associated with the pool of Israel, which is now paved over by a parking lot.

In the meantime, the biblical pool of Bethesda was lost until the late nineteenth century. The adjacent twelfth-century Church of St. Anne, though suffering from neglect, was sufficiently intact for the Ottoman Sultan Abdülmecid I (d. 1861) to offer the building and surrounding grounds to Emperor Napoleon III in 1856 as a gesture of gratitude for French support during the Crimean War. The architect Christophe-Edouard Mauss was sent in 1862 by the French government to restore the church. In 1873, he discovered the biblical site. The ruins of the small Crusader chapel were subsequent found in 1878. The pool of Bethesda epitomizes the "rediscovery" of the Holy Land that began in the nineteenth century and continues today. The site has been excavated by various teams throughout the late nineteenth and twentieth centuries and most recently from 1999–2009. Today, the Church of St. Anne remains the property of France and is one of four sites belonging to the *Domaine National Français en Terre Sainte*.[51]

Groups may hold a brief service of healing on the grounds around the archeological site. A modern pilgrim chapel, immediately north of the church, can also be booked (see website above). Consult denominational resources for liturgies and prayers.

PILGRIMAGE TEXTS: THE POOL OF BETHESDA

Eusebius, *Onomasticon* 59 (before 326): Bethesda (Bezatha): A bathing-pool in Jerusalem which is called *Probatike*, and formerly had five porticos. Now in the same place are shown twin pools, of which one is filled by the winter rains; in the other the water appears to have become red in an extraordinary way, a sign, they say, that in former times the priests purified themselves there. Because of this it is called *Probatike*, on account of the sacrifices.

---

50. *Second Guide* 6. While most twelfth-century maps locate the Probatica at St. Anne's, the Cambrai Map (c. 1150) places it at the pool of Israel.

51. On the pool of Bethesda and the Church of St. Anne, see Aist, *Christian Topography*; Pringle, *Churches*, 389–97; Schick, *Christian Communities*, 333–34; Murphy-O'Connor, *Holy Land*, 29–33.

The Stations

Eucherius, *Letter to Faustus* 8 (c. 430): Near the Temple is the Pool of Bethesda, distinguished by its twin pools. One is usually filled by winter rains, but the other is filled with dirty red water.

***Life of Peter the Iberian* r99 (c. 500):** From [the church called Pilate's] he went to the church of the Paralytic, and after that to Gethsemane.

Theodosius, *Topography of the Holy Land* 8b (c. 518): From the House of Pilate it is about 100 paces to the Sheep-Pool. There my Lord Christ cured the paralysed man, whose couch is still there. Beside the Sheep-Pool is the Church of my Lady Mary.

The Piacenza Pilgrim, *Travels* 27 (c. 570): We came to a bathing pool which has five porticos, one of which has the basilica of Saint Mary, where many miracles happen. This pool has now been reduced to excrement and all the city's undergarments are washed there. We saw in one dark corner the iron chain with which the unhappy Judas hanged himself.

Sophronius, *Anacreontica* 20.81–94 (before 614): Let me enter the holy Probatica, where the all-renowned Anna bore Mary. . . . May I behold that floor where the paralytic went at the behest of the Healing Word to lift his bed from the ground.

Hugeburc (Willibald), *Life of Willibald* 19 (724–26): [Willibald] went on to Solomon's porch [at the pool of Bethesda]. There is a pool, and sick people lie there waiting for the water to be moved, and for the angel to come and move the water: then the first to get down into it is cured. It is where the Lord said to the paralytic, "Arise, take up thy bed, and walk!"

SCRIPTURE READING: THE POOL OF BETHESDA

John 5:1–18: After this there was a festival of the Jews, and Jesus went up to Jerusalem. Now in Jerusalem by the Sheep Gate there is a pool, called in Hebrew Bethzatha, which has five porticoes. In these lay many invalids—blind, lame, and paralyzed. One man was there who had been ill for thirty-eight years. When Jesus saw him lying there and knew that he had been there a long time, he said to him, "Do you want to be made well?" The sick man answered him, "Sir, I have no one to put me into the pool when the water is stirred up; and while I am making my way, someone else steps down ahead of me." Jesus said to him, "Stand up, take your mat and walk." At once the man was made well, and he took up his mat and began to walk.

Now that day was a sabbath. So the Jews said to the man who had been cured, "It is the sabbath; it is not lawful for you to carry your mat." But he answered them, "The man who made me well said to me, 'Take up your mat and walk.'" They asked him, "Who is the man who said to you, 'Take it up and walk'?" Now the man who had been healed did not know who it was, for Jesus had disappeared in the crowd that was there. Later Jesus found him in the temple and said to him, "See, you have been made well! Do not sin any more, so that nothing worse happens to you." The man went away and told the Jews that it was Jesus who had made him well. Therefore the Jews started persecuting Jesus, because he was doing such things on the sabbath. But Jesus answered them, "My Father is still working, and I also am working." For this reason the Jews were seeking all the more to kill him, because he was not only breaking the sabbath, but was also calling God his own Father, thereby making himself equal to God.

Fig. 17. *The Pool of Bethesda*, 1839. The Pool of Israel prior to the rediscovery of biblical Bethesda. David Roberts (Scottish, 1796–1864). Colored lithograph. Credit: Wellcome Library, London. Wellcome Images, http://wellcomeimages.org, CC BY 4.0, via Wikimedia Commons.

Station 10
The Nativity of Mary

COMMEMORATING STATION 10: THE NATIVITY OF MARY

At the Church of St. Anne:

- Begin in prayer.
- Read the background information and pilgrimage texts for the nativity of Mary.
- Enter the church. Observe the simple beauty of the sanctuary (it was originally covered in frescoes).
- Visit the crypt marking the birthplace of Mary. What strikes you about the birth tradition of Mary?
- The church invites us to reflect upon three generations of the Holy Family. Speculate on Jesus' relationship to his grandparents. How has extended family been a part of your life journey?
- Listen to others sing in the church. Then sing as a group or solo.
- End in prayer.

BACKGROUND INFORMATION: THE NATIVITY OF MARY

Subsequently located at Bethesda, the tradition of Mary's Jerusalem birth appears in the *Protevangelium of James* (c. 200); according to the text, her father, Joachim, supplied sacrificial sheep for the temple.[52] The Byzantine church built over the Bethesda pools commemorated her birth; it was in ruins by the Crusader period. The twelfth-century Church of St. Anne was constructed immediately adjacent to the pools: the slight traces of Byzantine remains underneath the church are hard to interpret, and the existence of a previous church is uncertain. While commemorating the nativity of Mary, the church was formally dedicated to her mother, Anne. Following Saladin's conquest of Jerusalem, the church was converted on July 25, 1192, into a madrasa, an Islamic theological school, as we know from the inscription above the front central door. The building eventually fell into disuse and was abandoned in the early Ottoman period. The site was given to France in 1856 by the Ottomans in light of their support in the Crimean War and remains French national property.

The restored Romanesque church is known for its acoustics for Gregorian chant, and a popular practice of Jerusalem pilgrimage today is singing in the church, either as a group or solo. For the best effect, stand under the transept in front of the altar steps: sing slowly and controlled, softly but strong.

Upon entering the church, the sculpture on the left is Anne teaching her daughter, Mary, as she holds a scroll containing the words of the Shema from Deut 6:4–5: "Hear, O Israel: The Lord is our God, the Lord alone. You shall love the Lord your God with all your heart, and with all your soul, and with all your might." The stone altar in the center of the church is from 1950. The central panel depicts the annunciation of Mary, the nativity of Jesus, and Jesus' descent from the cross. The images on the sides of the altar are Mary being offered to the temple as a child (right) and Mary as an adult woman (left), both with her mother, Anne. High up on the supporting piers behind the altar are two small sculptures, slightly defaced, representing the Gospel writers of the nativity narratives of Jesus: an angel for Matthew (left) and an ox for Luke (right). The crypt of the church is dedicated to Mary's birth. The staircase is in the right-side aisle.

---

52. *Protevangelium of James* 4.

The Stations

PILGRIMAGE TEXTS: THE NATIVITY OF MARY

Theodosius, *Topography of the Holy Land* **8b (c. 518):** Beside the Sheep-Pool is the Church of my Lady Mary.

The Piacenza Pilgrim, *Travels* **27 (c. 570):** We came to a bathing pool which has five porticos, one of which has the basilica of Saint Mary, where many miracles happen.

Sophronius, *Anacreontica* **20.81–90 (before 614):** Let me enter the holy Probatica, where the all-renowned Anna bore Mary. And enter the church, church of the all-pure Mother of God, there in veneration to embrace those walls, so dear to me. Far be it from me, passing through the forum, to neglect the place where the Virgin Queen was born in noble palace!

Commemoratorium **8 (c. 808):** At St. Mary (where she was born at the Probatica) 5 [clergy], and 25 women dedicated to God as anchoresses.

The Protevangelium of James, **excerpts from 1–5 (c. 200):** The sons of Israel were bringing their gifts [to the Lord]. And Reubel stood up in front of [Joachim] and said, "It is not lawful for you to offer your gifts first, because you have begotten no offspring in Israel." Then Joachim became very sad, and went to the [record-book of the] twelve tribes of the people and said, to himself, "I will look in the register to see whether I am the only one who has not begotten offspring in Israel," and he searched and found that all the righteous had raised up offspring in Israel. And he remembered the patriarch Abraham to whom in his last days the Lord God gave a son, Isaac.

And Joachim was very sad, and did not show himself to his wife, but went into the wilderness; there he pitched his tent and fasted there forty days and forty nights, and said to himself: I Joachim shall not go down either for food or for drink until the Lord my God visits me; my prayer shall be food and drink.

Anna his wife sang two dirges and gave voice to a twofold lament: "I will mourn my widowhood, and grieve for my childlessness." . . . [And she] implored the Master saying, "O God of our fathers, bless me and heed my prayer, just as you blessed the womb of Sarah and gave her a son, Isaac." . . . And behold an angel of the Lord appeared to her and said, "Anna, Anna, the Lord God has heard your prayer. You shall conceive and bear, and your offspring shall be spoken of in the whole world." And Anna said, "As the

Lord my God lives, if I bear a child, whether male or female, I will bring it as a gift to the Lord God and it shall serve him all the days of its life."

And behold there came two angels, who said to her, "Behold, Joachim your husband is coming . . . for an angel of the Lord had come down to him and said to Joachim, 'Joachim, Joachim, the Lord God has heard your prayer. Go down from here; behold, your wife Anna shall conceive.'" . . . And her months were fulfilled; in the ninth month Anna gave birth. And she said to the midwife, "What have I brought forth?" And she said, "A female." And Anna said, "My soul is magnified this day." And she lay her down. And when the days were completed, Anna purified herself and gave suck to the child, and called her Mary.

Station 11
The Jephonias Monument

DIRECTIONS:
ST. ANNE'S TO THE JEPHONIAS MONUMENT

Leave St. Anne's and turn left. Exit the Old City through Lion's Gate, and immediately turn right (south). Enter the Muslim cemetery, taking the sidewalk approximately fifty meters or until you come to a suitable place overlooking Gethsemane.

Fig. 18. *The Dormition of the Virgin.* Ioannes Mokos (Greek, active 1680–1724). Tempera and oil on wood, gold ground. The Metropolitan Museum of Art. Open Access. Public domain.

THE STATION

No longer extant, the Jephonias monument, which marked an incident that occurred during Mary's funeral, was located outside the East Gate (Lion's Gate) overlooking the Jehoshaphat Valley and the Church of Mary's Tomb. The Muslim cemetery south of Lion's Gate is an appropriate place to commemorate the station.

COMMEMORATING STATION 11: THE JEPHONIAS MONUMENT

In the Muslim cemetery overlooking the Jehoshaphat Valley:

- Begin in prayer.
- Read the background information and pilgrimage texts for the Jephonias monument.
- How do you react to the Jephonias incident? Why would Christians erect a monument to remember the event?
- Think of contemporary monuments that commemorate events that are antagonistic toward other cultures, religions, or ethnic groups. What purpose or effect do they have?
- Consider the ethics of monumentalization. What power does a monument have?
- Reflect on the nature of funeral processions. What processions have you observed or participated in? What message, meaning, tone, or values do funeral processions convey?
- Read the Scripture readings for the Jehoshaphat Valley and the Mount of Olives: Joel 3:2 and Zech 14:4 (below).
- Look over the Jehoshaphat Valley ("Yahweh has judged") and the Mount of Olives. Note the massive cemeteries and individual tombs on both sides of the valley. All three Abrahamic faiths associate the setting with the end of time: e.g., the gathering of God's people, the return of prophets and messiahs, judgments and catastrophic events, redemption and resurrection. How are the holy sites of Jerusalem, including tombs, monuments of the future as much as the past?
- Say a prayer for the Other, and pray for the peace of Jerusalem.

The Stations

BACKGROUND INFORMATION: THE JEPHONIAS MONUMENT

To review the story, upon Mary's death on Mount Sion, the apostles carried her body to her tomb at Gethsemane in the Jehoshaphat Valley. On the way, the procession was interrupted by a Jew named Jephonias who attempted to steal Mary's body; however, his hands became fixed to the funeral bier as a sword-bearing angel severed his hands from his body. Jephonias repented, and his hands were restored. The confrontation is commonly depicted on Eastern Orthodox icons of Mary's dormition (see fig. 18).

Although the legend had been around for a couple of centuries, the monument first appears in the seventh century, and there is reason to suppose that it was erected during the short-lived Byzantine restoration following the Persian conquest. After retaining control of Jerusalem, the emperor Heraclius ordered reprisals against the local Jewish population, who had aided the Persians, including their expulsion from the city.[53] Jewish involvement in the Persian conquest may have incited Christians to build a monument that expressed anti-Jewish sentiment as well as eliciting Marian devotion.

The argument for dating the Jephonias monument to the Interconquest period is strengthened by another similarly shaped monument that also first appears in the seventh century; its context is the theme of the cross. Following the restoration of the Holy Cross by Heraclius, texts describe a monument associated with the healing powers of the Holy Cross near the eastern entrance of the Holy Sepulchre (see station 3). According to Christian tradition, Heraclius entered Jerusalem through the Golden Gate. In part, because the current gate is aligned with the Holy Sepulchre (not the Dome of the Rock), some scholars have proposed that it was constructed on the occasion of Heraclius's triumphal entrance.[54] In sum, Heraclius's restoration of the Holy Cross seems to have inspired commemorative activity in the city, including monuments dedicated to the miraculous healing of the Holy Cross (the Holy Sepulchre) and the Jephonias incident of Mary's funeral (outside the East Gate).[55]

---

53. Magness, *Jerusalem*, 344.

54. Magness, *Jerusalem*, 351.

55. See Aist, "Monument of the Miraculous Healing"; Aist, *Christian Topography*, 63–106, 165–74. Also see the pilgrim texts for station 3, esp. Adomnán and Epiphanius.

PILGRIMAGE TEXTS: THE JEPHONIAS MONUMENT

The Armenian Guide 6 (c. 630): Outside the city, at the place where the Jew snatched at the bier of the Holy Virgin and would not let her be buried, there is a dome resting on four marble columns and surmounted by a bronze cross.

Epiphanius, *Holy City* 24 (before 692): Outside the gate to the east of the Holy City stands a structure with four columns, in which Jephonias snatched at the bier of the most Holy Theotokos, and when he did not believe it belonged to the Lord's Mother his hands were cut off. And when he believed again, his hands were healed.

Hugeburc (Willibald), *Life of Willibald* 20 (724-26): There was a great column standing in front of the city gate, which had on top of it a cross as a sign to remind people of the place where the Jews wanted to take away the body of St. Mary. For as the eleven apostles were carrying the body of St. Mary and taking it down from Jerusalem, the moment they reached the city gate the Jews wanted to take it away. But any one of them who reached out to take hold of the bier found that his arms were trapped, and stuck to the bier as if they had been glued to it. They could not pull them free till, by the grace of God and the prayers of the apostles, they had been released. Then they left them alone.

Crusader Text: Daniel the Abbot, *Pilgrimage of Daniel the Monk* 21 (1106-8): It is 8 fathoms from the city gates to the place where the Jew [Jephonias] tried to cast down the body of the Holy Mother of God from her bier when the apostles were carrying her to be buried at Gethsemane, and the angel cut off both his hands with a sword and placed them on the bier.

SCRIPTURE READINGS: THE JEPHONIAS MONUMENT

The Jehoshaphat Valley and the Mount of Olives

Joel 3:2: I will gather all the nations and bring them down to the valley of Jehoshaphat, and I will enter into judgment with them there, on account of

The Stations

my people and my heritage Israel, because they have scattered them among the nations.

Zechariah 14:4: On that day his feet shall stand on the Mount of Olives, which lies before Jerusalem on the east; and the Mount of Olives shall be split in two from east to west by a very wide valley; so that half of the Mount shall withdraw northwards, and the other half southwards.

Station 12
The Church of Mary's Tomb

DIRECTIONS:
THE JEPHONIAS MONUMENT TO MARY'S TOMB

From Lion's Gate, follow the lane downhill until it ends. Turn right on Jericho Street. Cross Jericho Street at the traffic light. Continue on Jericho Street until you come to the Church of Mary's Tomb, which is in a sunken courtyard on the left. Descend by the steps on the left of the sidewalk.

Fig. 19. Detail of the Uppsala Map of Jerusalem, c. 1100–50. Gethsemane and the Church of Mary's Tomb on the left. Uppsala University Library, MS C 691, fol. 39v. Public domain.

The Stations

THE STATION

The Church of Mary's Tomb at Gethsemane. Upon entering the portal through the Crusader façade, continue down a flight of forty-five steps. Mary's tomb is on the right. The Church of Mary's Tomb is open daily from 6:30–12:30 and 14:00–18:00. Admission to the church is free. The closest free toilets are at the Mount of Olives Information Center on Jericho Street past the Church of Gethsemane.

COMMEMORATING STATION 12: MARY'S TOMB

In the courtyard of the Church of Mary's Tomb:

- Begin in prayer.
- Read the background information and pilgrimage texts for Mary's tomb.
- Review the dormition tradition of Mary (station 7).
- Enter the church, and slowly descend the stairs. Allow all five senses to be immersed in the setting. Explore the crypt, noting its icons and images.
- Enter the tomb of Mary. Stand or kneel beside the burial bench, which is protected by glass. Note the signs and offerings of previous pilgrims. Say a prayer.
- The tomb of Mary is venerated in Muslim tradition. Locate the mihrab in the south wall to the right of the tomb.
- View the icon of the All-Holy Lady of Jerusalem (the Jerusalem Virgin) in the east apse behind Mary's tomb.
- Observe the presence of other pilgrims and priests.
- Light a candle, if you wish.
- As you ascend the steps to exit the church, stop halfway up at the niche on left, which is dedicated to Mary's parents, Joachim and Anna. Take a moment to reflect upon the entirety of Mary's life from birth to death. What images and events from her life come to mind?
- The same niche formerly contained the tomb of Melisende, queen of Jerusalem (d. 1161). Women have played an important role in shaping

the Christian Holy Land. Remember the women of the Jerusalem Circuit. Say a prayer for Holy Land women today.

- End in prayer.

BACKGROUND INFORMATION: MARY'S TOMB

The Church of Mary's Tomb is accessed through a twelfth-century Crusader façade that immediately opens to a monumental staircase of forty-five steps that leads to the (lower) church, which is essentially a crypt. At the bottom of the steps on the right is Mary's tomb. Like the tomb of Christ, it has been cut away from the surrounding rock and isolated within the church. Other tombs in the crypt similar in style to first-century graves establish the site as an ancient cemetery (e.g., in the upper wall opposite the exit of Mary's tomb).

It is uncertain when the lower church, which is partially cut out of the bedrock, was first constructed, though the earliest date seems to be the fifth century. A story from the *Euthymiac History* (c. 550–c. 750), a problematic source as it only appears in other texts, tells how the emperor Marcian (d. 457) and his wife Pulcheria (d. 453) requested relics of the Virgin Mary from Juvenal, the patriarch of Jerusalem (d. 458), at the Council of Chalcedon in 451. Juvenal replied that three days after her burial, Mary's tomb was discovered to be empty, and her shroud was the only relic preserved in the church. The anecdote suggests that the Church of Mary's Tomb was built prior to 451. The first pilgrimage text to mention a church is the Piacenza Pilgrim (c. 570).

The complex also included an upper church built directly on top of the crypt. Described by Arculf (680s) as "remarkably round," the first upper church was probably constructed by Emperor Maurice (d. 602). Rebuilt by the Crusaders who found the upper church in ruins, Salah ed-Din destroyed it again in 1187, using its stone to repair sections of the city wall.

Despite the dismantling of the upper church, Mary's tomb has been venerated in Muslim tradition. According to Mujir al-Din (d. 1522), a Muslim scholar native to Jerusalem, Muhammed saw a light over the tomb of his "sister Mary" on his night journey to Jerusalem.[56] Mu'awiya (d. 680), the first Umayyad caliph, prayed at Mary's tomb in 660 when he was in Jerusalem for formal celebrations of his caliphate. There appears to be two

---

56. Mujir al-Din's own tomb is on street level in front of the church. He was formerly a student at the madrasa housed in the Church of St. Anne (station 10).

The Stations

mihrabs in the church: a small apse in the southern wall next to the entrance to Mary's tombs (mostly likely a former prayer niche) and one just inside the tomb itself. Today, Muslim pilgrims still frequent the site.

A more recent feature of the church is a modern icon of Mary and child located in the eastern apse behind the tomb. Known as the All-Holy Lady of Jerusalem (*Panagia Ierosolymitissa*), or simply the Jerusalem Virgin, the icon is considered by Orthodox Christians as the patroness of Jerusalem. The most common story of the icon's origins is that in 1870 Mary appeared as a stranger to a certain Sister Tatiana of the nearby Russian Convent of Mary Magdalene asking the sister to paint her image. Reluctant to do so, Tatiana woke up the next morning to discover the icon miraculously written: made without the help of human hands (*acheiropoieto*). As instructed by Mary, the icon was placed near her tomb.[57]

As you ascend the interior staircase to exit the church, halfway up on the left is a niche dedicated to Mary's parents, Anne and Joachim, which previously contained the tomb of Melisende (d. 1161), the Crusader queen of Jerusalem from 1131 until 1153. Queen Melisende was the eldest daughter of King Baldwin II (reigned 1118–31) and the wife of Fulk V of Anjou, king of Jerusalem from 1131–43. She was the mother of Kings Baldwin III (reigned 1143–63) and Amalric I (reigned 1163–74).

Finally, the Church of Mary's Tomb is a Status Quo site. The church belonged to the Franciscans from 1363 until 1757, when they lost possession to the Greeks, prompting the preliminary statement of the Status Quo that asserted the prerogative of the sultan to assign the sites as he pleased. Possession of the church is presently shared between the Greeks and the Armenians. While they both hold Eucharist every morning, they alternate days as custodians of the church. The Copts (twice a week) and the Syrian Orthodox (once a week) also have rights of usage. On Wednesday mornings, the Armenians, Copts, and Syrians simultaneously celebrate their respective liturgies using separate Armenian altars: the same occurs on Fridays but without the Syrians. The adjacent Grotto of Gethsemane remains in Franciscan hands.

---

57. There is a similar icon in the Church of the Nativity in Bethlehem in which Mary is slightly smiling. The history of the Bethlehem icon is uncertain.

PILGRIMAGE TEXTS: MARY'S TOMB

The Piacenza Pilgrim, *Travels* **17 (c. 570):** In that valley is the basilica of Saint Mary, which they say was her house, and from where she was taken up in body. This valley of Gethsemane is that same place that is called Jehoshaphat.

Sophronius, *Anacreontica* **20.95–100 (before 614):** Spiritual bliss will fill me when I hymn the glorious sanctuary of Gethsemane, which has received the body, the body of Mary, who gave birth to God. There they have built the tomb for the Mother of God.

Adomnán (Arculf), *On the Holy Places* **1.12 (680s):** The Church of Saint Mary in the Valley of Jehoshaphat . . . is built at two levels, and the lower part, which is beneath a stone vault, has a remarkable round shape. At the east end there is an altar, on the right of which is the empty rock tomb in which for a time Mary remained entombed. How or when, or by whom, her holy body was carried from this tomb, or where it awaits resurrection, no one, says Arculf, can be sure.

Hugeburc (Willibald), *Life of Willibald* **21 (724–26):** From there Bishop Willibald went down and came to the Valley of Jehoshaphat. It is situated next to the city of Jerusalem on the east. And in that valley is the Church of St. Mary, which contains her tomb—not because her body is buried there, but to commemorate her.

Commemoratorium **10 (c. 808):** In the valley of Jehoshaphat, at the village called Gethsemane, where St. Mary was buried and her tomb is venerated, 13 presbyters and clergy, 6 monks, 15 nuns who minister there.

Bernard, *Journey to the Holy Places* **13 (870):** Going outside Jerusalem we went down into the Valley of Jehoshaphat, a mile away from the city. . . . In this village there is also a round Church of St. Mary which contains her Tomb, but it has no roof and suffers from the rain.

Station 13
The Grotto of Gethsemane

DIRECTIONS:
MARY'S TOMB TO THE GROTTO OF GETHSEMANE

The Grotto of Gethsemane shares the same courtyard with the Church of Mary's Tomb. The grotto is at the end of a narrow exterior passageway on the right as you enter the courtyard (on the left as you exit the church).

The Kiss of Judas, Greek Chapel of Golgotha, Holy Sepulchre, Jerusalem.
Photo by Cole Yeoman. Used with permission.

THE STATION

The Grotto of Gethsemane, also known as the Grotto of the Apostles due to the tradition that the disciples often gathered there with Jesus, commemorates Jesus' betrayal and arrest. The Grotto of Gethsemane is open daily: 8:00–12:00 / 14:30–18:00, closing at 17:00 between October and March. Admission is free. If the site is closed, inquire at the Church of Gethsemane (station 14). The closest free toilets are at the Mount of Olives Information Center on Jericho Street past the Church of Gethsemane.

COMMEMORATING STATION 13: THE GROTTO OF GETHSEMANE

Group readings can be done in the courtyard before entering the grotto in silence. With permission from the Franciscan brother attending the site, group readings may also be done inside the grotto.

- Begin in prayer.
- Read the background information, pilgrimage texts, and Scripture readings for the Grotto of Gethsemane.
- Enter the grotto, observing its features, details, and images. Explore around the edges. Observe the Crusader designs on the ceiling.
- The grotto was a familiar base for Jesus and the disciples: a place where they ate, slept, talked, laughed, and argued. While sitting in the grotto, immerse yourself in the biblical setting. Entertain your religious imagination.
- Jesus takes three disciples away to pray. Imagine yourself as one of the disciples who remained in the grotto while Jesus was away.
- After Jesus returns to the cave, Judas arrives with a cohort of temple guards. You witness Jesus' betrayal and arrest. You see Peter resist by sword and hear Jesus' rebuke. You watch as they take Jesus away. Do you stay, flee, or follow?
- Reflect on the image of the kiss as a sign of betrayal.
- The encounter between Jesus and Nicodemus in John 3 may have occurred close to the grotto. Read the reflection near the doorway that recounts their conversation.
- End in prayer.

The Stations

BACKGROUND INFORMATION: THE GROTTO OF GETHSEMANE

The next two stations—the Grotto of Gethsemane and the Church of Gethsemane—belong to biblical Gethsemane, the setting of Jesus' prayer, betrayal, and arrest. The phrase "garden of Gethsemane" never appears in the Bible but is a conflation of scriptural references. Gethsemane is mentioned in Mark 14:32 and Matt 26:36, while John 18:1 refers to a garden on the other side of the Kidron Valley. Luke 22:39–40 sets the events at a place on the Mount of Olives. The details are enough to secure the location of biblical Gethsemane. From Jerusalem, Gethsemane was across the Kidron Valley, sufficiently above the valley floor to be regarded as the lower slope of the Mount of Olives.

Gethsemane means "oil press," and at the heart of Gethsemane is a natural cave that was used for pressing olives. We can imagine the site as a cultivated plot of ground, perhaps enclosed by a rock fence with the grotto serving as a sheltered place for producing olive oil. As olives were pressed in the autumn, the cave would have been available for temporary lodging during the spring festival of Passover when the city overflowed with pilgrims, and it's highly credible that the cave was used by Jesus and the disciples as a Jerusalem base. After the Passover meal inside the city, Jesus and the disciples returned to the shelter of a cave: a place well known to Judas as he had often been there with Jesus (John 18:2).

Although a cave is not mentioned in the Gospel accounts, it fits easily with the narrative and the wording of John's account. Jesus goes out from the cave to pray taking Peter, James, and John with him. After praying outside, he returns to the cave, where the rest of the disciples have remained. Knowing where Jesus would be, Judas arrives at the Gethsemane grotto with guards of the high priest. According to John 18:4, when the party approached, Jesus *came out* (*exēlthen*) to meet them. Although it doesn't demand it, the idea that Jesus came out from a cave may be implied by the text.

In any case, Jerusalem tradition associates the betrayal and arrest of Jesus with the grotto at Gethsemane.[58] While identifying the grotto as a church, pilgrim texts mention couches and tables where Jesus and the disciples ate and slept, which likely refer to stone apparatuses that were used in

---

58. At times in the Crusader and post-Crusader periods, the commemorations were switched: the grotto was identified with Jesus' prayer while the garden of the ruined church was the place of his arrest.

the pressing of olives. Despite its extramural location, the Theodosius text places the Last Supper in the grotto suggesting a minor alternative to Holy Sion (cf. Matt 26:18). The Crusader texts comment on the impression of Christ's fingers in the rock of the cave.

Access to the grotto is through an artificial entrance in its northwest corner that was opened in the Byzantine period. Long since blocked, the natural entrance to the cave, five meters in width, is to the north. The ceiling of the cave was plastered in the twelfth century and painted with eight-pointed stars. The cave with the land above it was purchased by the Franciscans in 1681–82. After a massive flood in November 1955, the cave was excavated by Father Virgilio Carbo prior to its restoration.[59]

PILGRIMAGE TEXTS: THE GROTTO OF GETHSEMANE

The Bordeaux Pilgrim, *Travels* 594 (333): When you have arrived at the gate of Jerusalem which faces the east, and are about to climb the Mount of Olives, there is what is called the Valley of Jehoshaphat. On your left, where there are vineyards, is a rock where Judas Iscariot betrayed Christ.

Theodosius, *Topography of the Holy Land* 10 (c. 518): The Valley of Jehoshaphat is there: there Judas betrayed my Lord: there is the Church of my Lady Mary, the Mother of the Lord: there also the Lord washed the disciples' feet and held the Supper: four couches are there in the place where my Lord reclined in the midst of the apostles, and each couch holds three men. Several of those who have come there for a religious reason like to eat food there (but not meat), and to light lamps where my Lord himself washed the apostles' feet. Also this place is in a cave, and two hundred monks go down there now.

The Piacenza Pilgrim, *Travels* 17 (c. 570): We came to the place in the valley of Gethsemane where the Lord was betrayed, in which there are three couches on which he reclined, and we reclined on them for a blessing.

Adomnán (Arculf), *On the Holy Places* 1.15 (680s): Not far above the Church of Saint Mary on the Mount of Olives there is a Cave which faces the Valley of Jehoshaphat. In it are two very deep wells: one goes down to an

---

59. Pringle, *Churches*, 98–103; Storme, *Gethsemane*.

untold depth below the mountain, and the other is in the floor of the cave: it has a huge shaft sunk deep, which goes down straight. Over these wells there is a permanent covering. This Cave also contains four rock tables. One of them which is just inside the entrance, is that of the Lord Jesus, and some times his seat was certainly beside this small table, on the frequent occasions when he used to recline there and have a meal, and the twelve Apostles reclined there with him at the other tables. The sealed mouth of the well which we described beneath the floor of the cave is to be seen closer to the tables of the Apostles. According to what holy Arculf says, this Cave has a small entrance which is closed by a wooden door, and he paid it many visits.

Bernard, *Journey to the Holy Places* **13 (870):** In that place there is also a church where the Lord was betrayed, and it contains four round tables at which he had supper.

Crusader Text: Belard of Ascoli, *Guide* **1 (c. 1155):** And in this garden [of Gethsemane] is a crypt dug into the rock of the Mount of Olives: this would take nearly three hundred people. And at the end of this crypt . . . Christ stood very often in prayer, and there he was captured. At its entrance there appears the shape of three fingers of his sacred hand, imprinted in the rock of the crypt, which, so it is said, he made when he was captured. This crypt is now a church.

SCRIPTURE READINGS: THE GROTTO OF GETHSEMANE

Matthew 26:47–56: While he was still speaking, Judas, one of the twelve, arrived; with him was a large crowd with swords and clubs, from the chief priests and the elders of the people. Now the betrayer had given them a sign, saying, "The one I will kiss is the man; arrest him." At once he came up to Jesus and said, "Greetings, Rabbi!" and kissed him. Jesus said to him, "Friend, do what you are here to do." Then they came and laid hands on Jesus and arrested him. Suddenly, one of those with Jesus put his hand on his sword, drew it, and struck the slave of the high priest, cutting off his ear. Then Jesus said to him, "Put your sword back into its place; for all who take the sword will perish by the sword. Do you think that I cannot appeal to my Father, and he will at once send me more than twelve legions of angels?

But how then would the Scriptures be fulfilled, which say it must happen in this way?" At that hour Jesus said to the crowds, "Have you come out with swords and clubs to arrest me as though I were a bandit? Day after day I sat in the temple teaching, and you did not arrest me. But all this has taken place, so that the Scriptures of the prophets may be fulfilled." Then all the disciples deserted him and fled.

John 18:1–12: After Jesus had spoken these words, he went out with his disciples across the Kidron valley to a place where there was a garden, which he and his disciples entered. Now Judas, who betrayed him, also knew the place, because Jesus often met there with his disciples. So Judas brought a detachment of soldiers together with police from the chief priests and the Pharisees, and they came there with lanterns and torches and weapons. Then Jesus, knowing all that was to happen to him, came forward and asked them, "Whom are you looking for?" They answered, "Jesus of Nazareth." Jesus replied, "I am he." Judas, who betrayed him, was standing with them. When Jesus said to them, "I am he," they stepped back and fell to the ground. Again he asked them, "Whom are you looking for?" And they said, "Jesus of Nazareth." Jesus answered, "I told you that I am he. So if you are looking for me, let these men go." This was to fulfill the word that he had spoken, "I did not lose a single one of those whom you gave me." Then Simon Peter, who had a sword, drew it, struck the high priest's slave, and cut off his right ear. The slave's name was Malchus. Jesus said to Peter, "Put your sword back into its sheath. Am I not to drink the cup that the Father has given me?" So the soldiers, their officer, and the Jewish police arrested Jesus and bound him.

Station 14
The Church of Gethsemane

DIRECTIONS:
THE GROTTO TO THE GETHSEMANE CHURCH

Leaving the courtyard of the Church of Mary's Tomb, ascend the steps on the left. At the top, proceed up the ramp to the T-junction, which is the intersection of al-Mansourieh Street and Jericho Road. Turn left up the lane (al-Mansourieh Street). The entrance to the site is on the right.

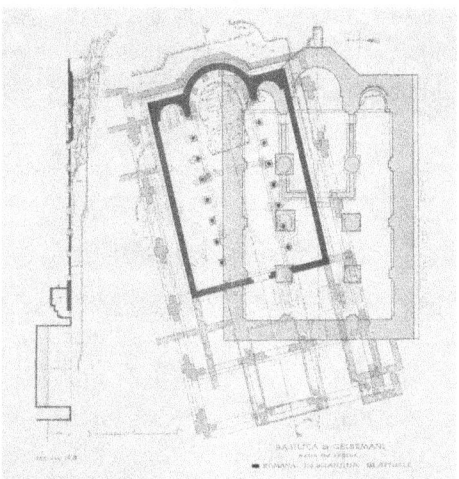

Fig. 21. The Basilica of Gethsemane. Antonio Barluzzi (Italian, 1884–1960). Adjusted key: Romana = Byzantine (fourth century); Bizantina = Crusader (twelfth century); Attuale = Current (twentieth century). With permission of the Historical Archive of the Custody of the Holy Land (ASCTS).

THE STATION

The Church of Gethsemane, formerly known as the Basilica of the Agony, is also called the Church of All Nations. A Franciscan site, the pilgrim area consists of a small olive grove and a modern church. The site is open daily from 8:00–18:00, closing at 17:00 between October and March. Admission is free. Slightly uphill from the entrance to the site, a set of pay toilets is occasionally open; the closest free toilets are at the Mount of Olives Information Center on Jericho Street across the road from the front of the church. See https://www.custodia.org/en/sanctuaries/gethsemane-basilica-agony.

COMMEMORATING STATION 14: THE CHURCH OF GETHSEMANE

Commence the station outside before entering the church in silence.

- Begin in prayer.
- Read the background information, pilgrimage texts, and Scripture readings for the Church of Gethsemane.
- Read the informational panels in the porch.
- Observe the olive trees in detail; eight are particularly old. In the pilgrim imagination, the trees function as silent witnesses to the Gethsemane events. What aspects of the story do the trees evoke? What wisdom could they share? Reflect on the concept of silent witness.
- Look west at the city walls. Glimpse the top of the Dome of the Rock; the Herodian temple was taller. Reflect on Jesus' prayer in the garden in light of Gethsemane's proximity to the temple.
- Observe the exterior features of the church. How do they convey the themes of Gethsemane? Are any of the images surprising?
- Note how the front doors convey a sense of entering an olive grove. Find the Latin inscription above the doorway: *Sustinete Hic Et Vigilate Mecum*: "Stay here and keep watch with me" (Matt 26:38). What thoughts and emotions do the words evoke? Receive them as an invitation to prayerfully enter the church.
- Observe the interior details of the church. Survey the mosaic ceiling depicting the night sky. Feel the mood cast by the purple windows.

- Contemplate the three mosaics in the apse of the church. How is the one on the left different from the one on the right?
- Approach the rock that commemorates the place of Jesus' prayer. Observe the sculpture of the crown of thorns surrounding the rock. How is our understanding of Gethsemane framed by the crucifixion?
- Find a place to kneel or sit. Pray in silence, allowing the setting and the story to converge.
- End in prayer.

BACKGROUND INFORMATION: THE CHURCH OF GETHSEMANE

Few Christian narratives have more iconic phrases than Jesus' agony in Gethsemane: "The spirit is willing; the body is weak. . . . Remove this cup from me. . . . Not my will but yours be done. . . . I am deeply grieved, even to death. . . . Remain here, and stay awake with me."

The Gethsemane church incorporates the rock where Jesus purportedly prayed the night before his passion.[60] Jesus died on a cross at Golgotha, but Gethsemane was the crucible, the final test, the place where Jesus' mission, purpose, and identity converged into a single faithful act: Jesus stayed. Unlike King David who fled the city via the Mount of Olives, Jesus remained (2 Sam 15:30).

In his entry for Gethsemane in the *Onomasticon*, which is dated before Constantine's involvement in the Holy Land,[61] Eusebius writes without mentioning a church: "Gethsemane: A place where Christ prayed before the Passion. It is right by the Mount of Olives, in which even now the faithful are zealous in offering prayers." The Byzantine Church of Gethsemane was built by Emperor Theodosius (d. 395) sometime between 379 and 384. In his Latin translation of the *Onomasticon*, written in 388, Jerome adds the phrase, "It is at the foot of the Mount of Olives where now a church has been built," while Egeria, in the same decade, refers to an "elegant church" at the place where Jesus prayed.[62]

---

60. See Murphy-O'Connor, "What Really Happened at Gethsemane?"

61. Taylor dates the text between 313 and mid-325, but no later; see Freeman-Grenville, *Palestine in the Fourth Century*, 3.

62. Eusebius, *Onomasticon*, 74; Jerome, *Book of Places*, 75; Egeria, *Travels* 36.1.

There is uncertainty about the site during the Early Islamic period. In short, one must reconcile Willibald's reference to a church at the place of Jesus' prayer, the last mention of a church commemorating the agony before the Crusades, with the evidence that the Byzantine church was destroyed by fire. Most scholars assume that the fire was associated with the Persian conquest in 614. This would necessitate the rebuilding of the church prior to Willibald's visit in 724–26, which could be explained by Modestus's restoration of churches following the conquest. The fire has also been linked to the earthquake of 749, or some twenty years after Willibald's travels. The later date would allow for the church.[63]

We should assume that Willibald visited the Byzantine site. However, a number of scholars have suggested that Willibald—and later Bernard, who doesn't mention a church—is referring to a site farther up the Mount of Olives. The question takes into account liturgical factors as well as descriptions of the mountain, which are not easy to interpret. While it's possible, the argument that the location moved—and then moved back again in the Crusader period—is not convincing. A more intriguing alternative, if one is needed, is that Willibald's church is the Grotto of Gethsemane: a possibility strengthened by Arculf's report (680s), which locates the stone of the agony just meters away in the Church of Mary's Tomb (see below). If the displaced stone is a sign of the discontinuity of the Gethsemane church, it also suggests that the commemoration of Jesus' prayer remained with the Gethsemane sites and did moved up the mountain.[64]

The continuity of the site is ultimately supported by subsequent Crusader activity, which placed a small oratory at Gethsemane within months of their arrival before eventually constructing a larger church (c. 1170). If the Crusaders knew where the Byzantine location was, then Willibald and Bernard certainly did: at least, the *memory* of the Byzantine site was never lost, even if a surrogate site was temporary used.

Aligned to the east, the Crusader structure corrected a pronounced misorientation of the Byzantine church; it incorporated, however, much of the same rock associated with Jesus' prayer, underscoring the continuity of tradition between the periods. Both were double-aisled basilicas with three apses (see fig. 21). Although pilgrimage texts up until 1323 continue to

---

63. On destruction by earthquake, see Murphy-O'Connor, *Holy Land*, 147.

64. The respective views of Willibald's church are discussed in Aist, *Christian Topography*, 194–202, and Limor, "Origins of a Tradition," 460–62. Also see Schick, *Christian Communities*, 351–53; Pringle, *Churches*, 98, 358–59.

refer to the church, the post-Crusader evidence is inconsistent. The church may have been destroyed soon after 1187 when Saladin repaired the city walls, while in 1192 the property appears to have been given to the madrasa recently established at St. Anne's. The site was definitely in ruins by the end of the fourteenth century.

Purchased by three brothers from Sarajevo, the Franciscans acquired the property on May 2, 1681. Excavations commenced in the late nineteenth century, and the ruins of the Crusader church were found in 1909. Antonio Barluzzi (d. 1960), known as the modern architect of the Holy Land, was commissioned to design a new church oriented upon the Crusader foundations, the first of his Holy Land churches: the foundation stone was laid in October 1919. Initial borings of the site led workers to believe that the Crusader church had been built directly on top of the Byzantine basilica. However, the actual Byzantine structure was soon discovered two meters lower than the Crusader church. It was oriented, as mentioned, at a different angle. The project was stopped; further excavations were made, and the church was recommenced along the Byzantine lines. Work continued from April 1922 until the new Basilica of the Agony was consecrated on June 15, 1924; it is also known as the Church of All Nations, as several countries donated to the cost of the building.

On top of the church are two stags adoring the cross (the stag is an ancient symbol of Christ). The large mosaic on the pediment (front façade) is by Giulio Bargellini (d. 1954). Christ stands in the center as judge. On the left are the poor and lowly who look to Christ in faith. On the right, the powerful and wealthy stand in shame, aware of their sins. A 1924 statement by the Custody of the Holy on the construction of the church captures the intended message of the mosaic: "After centuries of abandonment due to quarrels between men, [God] wants the Shrine that celebrates the greatest of sufferings . . . to rise again as a warning and as a comfort to all [people] who seek the secret of peace." Below the mosaic, the marble statues sculpted by Giuseppe Tonnini (d. 1954) depict the Gospel writers holding open books with Gethsemane Scriptures—from left to right: Mark, Luke, Matthew, and John. The eight oldest olive trees in the garden, though unlikely to be more than a few hundred years old(!), are extremely evocative, playing the role of silent witness to Jesus' agony in the garden. On the other side of the church, extending beyond the eastern end of the southern wall, part of the Crusader foundation can still be seen.

Inside, the church is meant to evoke a mood of overwhelming depression and agony, which is conveyed by the simulation of a nighttime setting enhanced by the relatively low level of the dark blue ceiling. Adding to the effect are the dimly lit windows made of violet alabaster. According to Barluzzi, if the church facilitates "the weeping of the faithful souls on the suffering of Christ, it will have reached the apex of artistic success."[65]

Along with the front doors that convey a sense of entering an olive grove, images of olive branches can be found on the ceiling of the church. Surrounding the rock of agony in front of the altar, the iron sculpture of the crown of thorns, executed by Alberto Gerardi (d. 1965), consists of olive branches with pairs of birds and chalices representing the souls that drink the blood of Christ; the injured doves in the corners are symbols of suffering. Above the rock, the golden mosaic in the cupola is decorated with four angels and symbols of salvation, while the dark blue ceiling mosaic depicts starry skies, olive trees, palm trees, and the coats of arms of the nations that helped finance the church. The three apse mosaics convey the events of Gethsemane. In the middle, *The Agony of Jesus* by Pietro D'Achiardi (d. 1940) shows Jesus in prayer as an angel descends from heaven to comfort him while the disciples sleep (Luke 22:43). The two side mosaics, both by Mario Barberis (d. 1960), illustrate scenes of the betrayal and arrest of Jesus. On the left, *The Kiss of Judas* follows the synoptic tradition of Judas betraying Jesus with a kiss (Matt 26; Mark 14; Luke 22); John doesn't mention a kiss. On the right, the mosaic, *Ego Sum*, portrays the Johannine version of Jesus' betrayal: "When Jesus said to them, 'I am he,' they stepped back and fell to the ground" (John 18:6). The floor pavement marks the walls, columns, and mosaic patterns of the Byzantine structure, which was smaller than the present-day church.[66]

---

65. The two quotes appeared on panels displayed at the 2024 exhibition of the Custody of the Holy Land: LUXTENEBRA: 100 Years Since the Building of the Basilica of the Agony.

66. The discussion makes use of Panzetta and Monicolini, *Italian Artists*, 18–23; Pringle, *Churches*, 358–65; Murphy-O'Connor, *Holy Land*, 146–48; Schick, *Christian Communities*, 351–53; Aist, *Christian Topography*, 194–202. Also see Storme, *Gethsemane*.

PILGRIMAGE TEXTS:
THE CHURCH OF GETHSEMANE

Adomnán (Arculf), *On the Holy Places* 1.12 (680s): Entering the lower round Church of Saint Mary one sees on the right, let into the wall, a rock. On it the Lord knelt to pray in the field of Gethsemane just before he was betrayed, on the night when he was "given up into the hands of wicked men" and to Judas. The marks of his knees are visible, printed deeply in this rock, as if it had been soft wax.

Hugeburc (Willibald), *Life of Willibald* 21 (724-26): There is now a church on the Mount of Olives at the place where, before his Passion, the Lord prayed, and said to his disciples, "Watch and pray, so that you do not enter into temptation."

Bernard, *Journey to the Holy Places* 13 (870): Going outside Jerusalem we went down into the Valley of Jehoshaphat, a mile away from the city, which contains the village of Gethsemane. . . . In that place there is also a church where the Lord was betrayed, and it contains four round tables at which he had supper. . . . From this we hurried on to the Mount of Olives, on the lower slopes of which we were shown the place where the Lord made his prayer to the Father.

SCRIPTURE READINGS:
THE CHURCH OF GETHSEMANE

Matthew 26:36-46: Then Jesus went with them to a place called Gethsemane; and he said to his disciples, "Sit here while I go over there and pray." He took with him Peter and the two sons of Zebedee, and began to be grieved and agitated. Then he said to them, "I am deeply grieved, even to death; remain here, and stay awake with me." And going a little farther, he threw himself on the ground and prayed, "My Father, if it is possible, let this cup pass from me; yet not what I want but what you want." Then he came to the disciples and found them sleeping; and he said to Peter, "So, could you not stay awake with me one hour? Stay awake and pray that you may not come into the time of trial; the spirit indeed is willing, but the flesh is weak." Again he went away for the second time and prayed, "My Father, if this cannot pass unless I drink it, your will be done." Again he came and found them sleeping, for their eyes were heavy. So leaving them again, he went away and prayed for the third time, saying the same words. Then he came to the disciples and said to them, "Are you still sleeping and taking your rest? See, the hour is at hand, and the Son of Man is betrayed into the hands of sinners. Get up, let us be going. See, my betrayer is at hand."

Luke 22:39–46: [Jesus] came out and went, as was his custom, to the Mount of Olives; and the disciples followed him. When he reached the place, he said to them, "Pray that you may not come into the time of trial." Then he withdrew from them about a stone's throw, knelt down, and prayed. "Father, if you are willing, remove this cup from me; yet, not my will but yours be done." Then an angel from heaven appeared to him and gave him strength. In his anguish he prayed more earnestly, and his sweat became like great drops of blood falling down on the ground. When he got up from prayer, he came to the disciples and found them sleeping because of grief, and he said to them, "Why are you sleeping? Get up and pray that you may not come into the time of trial."

2 Samuel 15:30 (David flees from Jerusalem): But David went up the ascent of the Mount of Olives, weeping as he went, with his head covered and walking barefoot; and all the people who were with him covered their heads and went up, weeping as they went.

Station 15
The Eleona

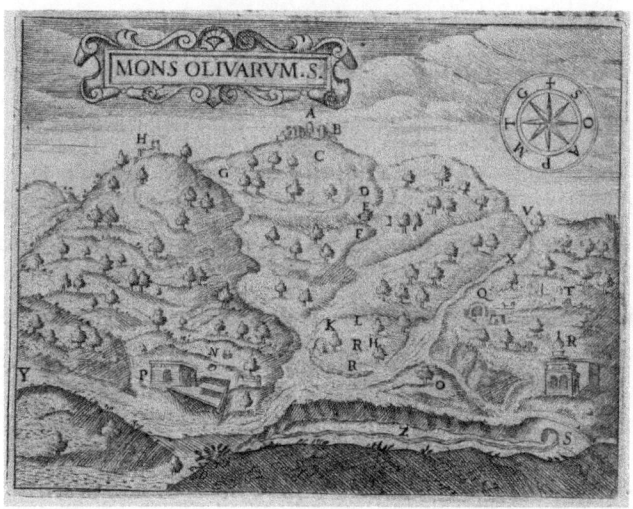

Fig. 22. *Mons Olivarum.s* (The Mount of Olives), 1587. Jean Zuallart (Belgium, 1541–1634). Copperplate. The Eran Laor Map Cartographic Collection. The National Library of Israel. Public domain.

DIRECTIONS:
GETHSEMANE TO THE ELEONA

From Gethsemane, the way to the Eleona involves a climb up the Mount of Olives. The recommended route is a pedestrian sidewalk of five hundred steps. Leaving the Church of Gethsemane, turn right onto al-Mansourieh

Street. Continue past the lane on the right for approximately thirty meters until you come to the sidewalk that leads up the mountain: it is located between the tarmac roads. Upon reaching the top of the steps, continue straight, merging with the road ahead. The entrance to the Eleona is on the right at the T-junction.

As an alternative route, take the tarmac lane that runs behind the back of the Gethsemane church. Follow the road to nearly the top of the ridge, where it makes a ninety-degree turn to the right. Continue straight up the flight of steps immediately ahead. At the top of the steps, take the road to the left. Go approximately 250 meters—the road eventually bends to the right—until you come to the entrance of the Eleona on your right. Be aware of pickpockets who present themselves as street vendors selling horizon photos of Jerusalem (see section 2).

THE STATION

The Eleona ("of olives") on the Mount of Olives is also known as the Church of the Pater Noster, as it has commemorated Jesus' teaching of the Lord's Prayer since the Crusader period. At the time of the Jerusalem Circuit, the church remembered Jesus' discourse on the end of time. The Eleona is open Monday–Saturday from 8:00–12:00 and 14:00–17:00. It is closed on Sundays as well as Christmas and New Year. Admission to the site is 10 NIS. Students are 8 NIS. There are free toilets at the church. Consult the gift shop for the location of languages displayed throughout the site.

COMMEMORATING STATION 15: THE ELEONA

Commemorate the Eleona at various locations throughout the site, including the grotto, the grounds of the unfinished church, the partial cloister, the nineteenth-century chapel, and the olive garden overlooking Jerusalem.

- Begin in prayer.
- Read the background information, pilgrimage texts, and Scripture readings for the Eleona.
- Visit the grotto underneath the altar area of the unfinished church. This is one of the three mystic caves mentioned by Eusebius.

- Visit the olive grove. As you look over the city of Jerusalem, reread the Apocalyptic Discourse (Mark 13). Reflect on the reading from the viewpoint of the disciples and the early church.
- Reflect on the Apocalyptic Discourse from the perspective of Byzantine Christians. Why was the commemoration important?
- Reflect upon the texts from the vantage point of the modern church. A comprehensive treatment of Holy Week must take into account the Apocalyptic Discourse. Why is it a difficult set of texts?
- Why do you think Jesus' teaching about the end of time was eventually replaced by the Lord's Prayer?
- Look over the translations of the Lord's Prayer throughout the site, ideally with another person exploring the languages together. What languages are you familiar with or have a connection to? Which ones surprise you? Are there people with you who speak a language different from you? Invite them to pray their version of the Lord's Prayer out loud.
- Feel the Pentecost-like atmosphere of the place. You are a part of Holy Land tradition, past and present, comprised of pilgrims representing languages and cultures from around the globe. Say the Lord's Prayer remembering the needs of the world.
- As you walk the site, observe the behaviors and emotions of other pilgrims. What countries are they from?
- Spend time in the gift shop looking through the postcards and plaques of the Lord's Prayer in nearly two hundred languages.
- End in prayer.

BACKGROUND INFORMATION: THE ELEONA

The grotto at the Eleona marks the place in Christian tradition where Jesus taught the disciples concerning the end of time, the so-called Apocalyptic Discourse (Mark 13, Matt 24, and Luke 21) that took place on the Mount of Olives during the final week of his life. Topics included the destruction of Jerusalem and the end of the world. Christians adopted the Jewish belief that God's judgment would take place on the slopes of the Mount of Olives when the nations would be gathered below in the Jehoshaphat Valley (see Joel 3:2; Zech 14:4).

The area was also associated with the promise of Jesus' return, emphasizing the eschatological importance of the Mount of Olives. Indeed, Eusebius connects the cave with Jesus' ascension. According to Eusebius, there were three mystic caves upon which Constantine founded his first Holy Land churches: the Holy Sepulchre (the tomb of Christ), the Church of the Nativity in Bethlehem (the grotto of Jesus' birth), and the Eleona (the grotto of the ascension).[67] It was theologically fitting that the first three Constantinian churches commemorated the salvific events of the nativity, resurrection, and ascension of Christ. But, of course, the ascension doesn't lend itself to a cave. As noted by the Bordeaux Pilgrim as early as 333, Jesus' teaching of the end times emerged as the primary memory of the Eleona, while the place of the ascension was eventually moved to a purpose-built church approximately fifty meters away (see station 16).

A landmark church of the Byzantine period, the Eleona was a significant station of the Jerusalem liturgy, serving, for instance, as the beginning point for the Palm Sunday procession. It was also the burial place for a number of Jerusalem bishops, including Cyril of Jerusalem (d. 386).

The church was seriously damaged by the Persians in 614. Although it continued in use, the site was eclipsed in the Early Islamic period by the nearby Church of the Ascension. Adomnán refers to the Eleona as "another famous church," though it's unclear whether Arculf reports this or if Adomnán is using an earlier source. More certain, Epiphanius (before 692) describes the site, while the ninth-century *Commemoratorium* states that the church where Christ taught his disciples on the Mount of Olives was administered by three monks and one priest. The Eleona is also mentioned in the *Georgian Calendar* (tenth century or earlier). Notwithstanding the physical condition of the church (it was in ruins when the Crusaders arrived), there was a Christian presence at the site during the Early Islamic period retaining the memory of the Eleona as a place where Jesus taught.[68]

But what did Jesus teach? The Crusaders rebuilt the church in the twelfth century; however, the contents of Jesus' teaching changed from the Apocalyptic Discourse to the Lord's Prayer, which remains the commemoration today (see Saewulf below). While Luke places the Lord's Prayer in the

---

67. Eusebius, *In Praise of Constantine* 9.16–17.

68. Schick, *Christian Communities*, 350–51, which includes references to the *Georgian Calendar*.

The Stations

general area of Jerusalem (Luke 10:38—11:4; cf. Matt 5–7), its association with the Eleona is somewhat strained, particularly compared to the Apocalyptic Discourse that explicitly took place on the Mount of Olives.

The Crusader church was severely damaged during Saladin's reconquest of Jerusalem in 1187, and the site lay in ruins until the modern period. The site was purchased in 1856 by Aurélie de Bossi, the princess of La Tour d'Auvergne (d. 1889), who built a convent for contemplative Carmelite sisters, including a chapel and cloister, which was completed in 1874. Modeled on the Campo Santo in Pisa, Italy, the Gothic cloister was inspired by the famous French architect Eugène Viollet-le-Duc (d. 1879). Unbeknownst in the planning, the buildings were constructed over the eastern end of the former Constantinian church (which may have been discovered at the time). Excavations carried out in 1910 revealed the foundations of the fourth-century church, together with the grotto. Construction of a replica church on the original Byzantine footing was started in 1920, requiring the destruction of the western wall of the cloister. The project was abandoned in 1927 due to a lack of funds, leaving an open cloister and an unfinished church, which would have been dedicated to the Sacred Heart of Jesus (Sacré Coeur).

The original property now has three separate owners. In 1868, the princess of La Tour d'Auvergne gave part of the site to France—essentially the pilgrim area today minus the olive tree garden to the south. Along with St. Anne's (stations 9–10), the Eleona is one of four properties owned by the *Domaine National Français en Terre Sainte*. What is now the olive tree garden was given to the White Fathers in 1883; it was opened to pilgrims for prayer and meditation in 2011. The Carmelite sisters, who are the spiritual guardians of the site, own the grounds of their convent.[69]

Today, the Eleona displays the Lord's Prayer on ceramic tiles in nearly two hundred languages, and there is an application process for additional languages. Other than a framed print in the gift shop, there is little-to-no mention of the site's former memory, Jesus' discourse on the end of time, though signage could change in the future. For now, guides almost exclusively interpret the grotto as the place where Jesus taught the Lord's Prayer. That said, Pater Noster offers a powerful Pentecost-like experience of hearing the wonders of God in each our own language (Acts 2). The site celebrates the rich linguistic and cultural diversity of the Christian faith that has spread from Jerusalem to the ends of the world.

---

69. Pringle, *Churches*, 121; Murphy-O'Connor, *Holy Land*, 143–44.

Walking the Jerusalem Circuit

PILGRIMAGE TEXTS: THE ELEONA

Bordeaux Pilgrim, *Travels* **595 (333):** On the Mount of Olives, where the Lord taught before his passion, a basilica has been built by command of Constantine.

Eucherius, *Letter to Faustus* **10 (c. 430):** And on the east the city looks out at the Mount of Olives. On this there are two very famous churches, one sited at the spot where Jesus addressed his disciples, and the other at the spot where it is said that he ascended into heaven.

Sophronius, *Anacreontica* **19.5-16 (before 614):** Highly will I praise the endless depth of the divine Wisdom, by which he saved me, swiftly will I pass thence to the place, [w]here, to his venerable companions he taught the divine mysteries shedding light into secret depths, there, under the roof, may I be! Then let me go out through the Great Door onto the steps, and regard the beauty of the Holy City lying over to the west.

Epiphanius, *Holy City* **33 (before 692):** And further on to the east there are 2,340 steps going up to the Place of Teaching in which Christ taught the apostles saying, "I am about to be taken up. And as for you, go and teach the things I have taught you." Not far to the north of the Place of Teaching is a church, in the middle of which is the stone where Christ stood when he was taken up.

Commemoratorium **24 (c. 808):** [On] the holy Mount of Olives. . . . The Church Where Christ Taught his Disciples, 3 monks, 1 presbyter.

Crusader Text: Saewulf, *Pilgrimage of Saewulf* **18 (1101-3):** A stone's throw away from [the place of the Ascension] our Lord wrote the Lord's Prayer with his own hands upon the rock, in Hebrew, so the Assyrians state. There was a very beautiful church there, but later it had been totally destroyed by the pagans.

SCRIPTURE READINGS: THE ELEONA

Mark 13:3-32 (also see Matthew 24 and Luke 21): When [Jesus] was sitting on the Mount of Olives opposite the temple, Peter, James, John, and Andrew asked him privately, "Tell us, when will this be, and what will be the sign that all these things are about to be accomplished?" Then Jesus began to say to them, "Beware that no one leads you astray. Many will come in my name and say, 'I am he!' and they will lead many astray. When you hear of wars and rumors of wars, do not be alarmed; this must take place, but the end is still to come. For nation will rise against nation, and kingdom against kingdom; there will be earthquakes in various places; there will be famines. This is but the beginning of the birth pangs. . . . And the good news must first be proclaimed to all nations. When they bring you to trial and hand you over, do not worry beforehand about what you are to say; but say whatever is given you at that time, for it is not you who speak, but the Holy Spirit. Brother will betray brother to death, and a father his child, and children will rise against parents and have them put to death; and you will be hated by all because of my name. But the one who endures to the end will be saved. But when you see the desolating sacrilege set up where it ought not to be (let the reader understand), then those in Judea must flee to the mountains; the one on the housetop must not go down or enter the house to take anything away; the one in the field must not turn back to get a coat. Woe to those who are pregnant and to those who are nursing infants in those days! Pray that it may not be in winter. For in those days there will be suffering, such as has not been from the beginning of the creation that God created until now, no, and never will be. And if the Lord had not cut short those days, no one would be saved. . . . And if anyone says to you at that time, 'Look! Here is the Messiah!' or 'Look! There he is!'—do not believe it. False messiahs and false prophets will appear and produce signs and omens, to lead astray, if possible, the elect. But be alert; I have already told you everything. But in those days, after that suffering, the sun will be darkened, and the moon will not give its light, and the stars will be falling from heaven, and the powers in the heavens will be shaken. Then they will see 'the Son of Man coming in clouds' with great power and glory. Then he will send out the angels, and gather his elect from the four winds, from the ends of the earth to the ends of heaven. . . . Truly I tell you, this generation will not pass away until all these things have taken place. Heaven and earth will pass away, but my words will not pass away. But about that day or hour no one knows, neither the angels in heaven, nor the Son, but only the Father. Beware, keep alert; for you do not know when the time will come."

Station 16
The Church of the Ascension

DIRECTIONS:
THE ELEONA TO THE ASCENSION

Upon leaving the Eleona, take the crosswalk to the right and proceed up the street for approximately seventy meters. The Chapel of the Ascension is on the right.

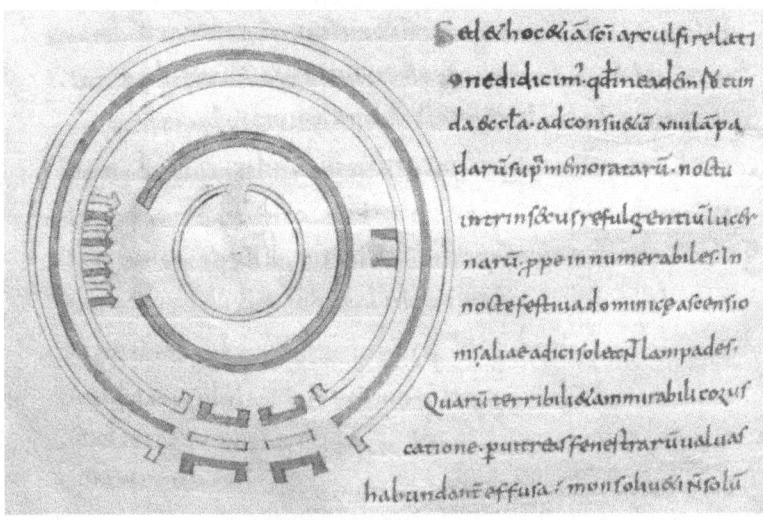

Fig. 23. The Church of the Ascension. Vienna, Österreichische Nationalbibliothek, Cod. 458, fol. 11v. Ninth-century manuscript drawing based on the late seventh-century prototype in Adomnán, *De locis sanctis*. Used with permission.

The Stations

THE STATION

The Chapel of the Ascension is on the grounds of the former Byzantine church. The site is open daily approximately from 8:00–17:00. It may be briefly closed during times of Muslim prayer. If so, wait a few minutes until a custodian appears. Admission to the site is 10 NIS. Ask for directions for nearby public toilets.

COMMEMORATING STATION 16: THE ASCENSION

Commemorate the station inside the chapel and around the grounds. Groups may read, pray, and sing in the chapel, monitoring their time with respect to others waiting to enter.

- Begin in prayer.
- Read the background information, pilgrimage texts, and Scripture readings for the place of the ascension.

Inside the chapel:

- The rock framed on the floor purportedly contains the right footprint of Jesus. The foot points to the north, or to the left as you enter. Observe, touch, kiss, or measure the footprint, and light a candle, if desired.
- Use Jesus' last footprint as a means to reflect upon his earthly life from annunciation to ascension.
- Note the mihrab for Muslim prayer.
- Groups may sing a brief hymn.

On the grounds outside the chapel:

- Spend time in the open grounds of the site. This was originally the interior of the roofless church. Reread the narratives from Luke and Acts as you look into the skies of the ascension event.
- Recall the words of the men dressed in white robes who said that Jesus would return in the same way that he was taken up into heaven. They were commemorated by two columns in the eighth century. Reread the Willibald passage.

- Most Holy Land shrines invite us to look down on the ground or to imagine a biblical scene within the confines of an enclosed church. The place of the ascension beckons us to follow the story by looking up into the sky while heeding the message of the men in white. What did their words mean to past pilgrims? What do they signify for Christians today? How is the ascension site a place of creative tension?

- A Christian shrine has been described as a place that evokes God's presence in the past, the present, and the future.[70] How is this especially true for the place of the ascension?

- Observe the details of the Crusader capitals on the exterior walls of the chapel.

- The site has been in Muslim hands since the end of the Crusader period. Muslims believe that Jesus ascended into heaven as a living person (someone was crucified, but it wasn't Jesus). Muslims also believe that Jesus will return. While acknowledging important differences, consider the ascension as a place of convergence for Christians and Muslims.

- The Chapel of the Ascension is a Status Quo site, and five Christian communities are granted the right of liturgical usage on their respective feasts of the ascension. Note their respective altars. Reread the Arculf passage about the noonday wind.

- Reflect on the Chapel of the Ascension as a *shared* (interfaith, ecumenical) site rather than a *contested* one.

- Today, only a small percentage of Christian pilgrims visit the ascension site: it is not included on the majority of pilgrim itineraries. Why might this be the case? What does the Christian Holy Land experience lose by omitting the place of the ascension?

- Exit the site and look over the city of Jerusalem (erase the buildings across the street from your mind). Reread the description of Arculf, describing the ascension lamps. Imagine the lamps illuminating the valley, connecting the place of the ascension with the city of Jerusalem.

- End in prayer.

---

70. See Inge, *Christian Theology*, 103–22.

THE STATIONS

BACKGROUND INFORMATION: THE ASCENSION

Sometime before 392, a church dedicated to the ascension was constructed just north of the Eleona at a slightly more elevated place, known as the Imbomon ("the hillock"), on the same ridge of the Mount of Olives overlooking Jerusalem. The church was financed by Poimenia, a female member of the imperial family. According to Adomnán's seventh-century drawing of the building (see fig. 23), the main entrance of the church was on the south; thus, it faced the Eleona, shortening the distance between the churches.

The pre-Crusader site emphasized two commemorative features: (1) the last footprints of Jesus, and (2) the open skies of the ascension event. The footprints marked the final bodily contact that Jesus had with earth, inviting reflection on the entirety of Jesus' life as well as his future return. The alleged right footprint of Jesus is still shown today. As for the skies, the Byzantine church was built as a circular structure without a roof, allowing pilgrims to gaze into the heavens of Jesus' ascent.

Today, the grounds essentially correspond with the open interior of the round Byzantine church, which was supported by radiating buttresses: concentric walls were vaulted as porticos and an eastern apse enclosed the site. Surrounded by a railing and illuminated with hanging lamps, the footprints of Jesus were at the center of the roofless church (see fig. 23). Therefore, pilgrims could visually trace the ascension event from the ground to the sky. While churches on the Mount of Olives suffered damage—and were variously restored—during the transitional years of the Persian and Arab conquests, pilgrims of the Early Islamic period experienced the Church of the Ascension as a place of particular importance and religious imagination, as witnessed by Arculf and Willibald.

During the Crusader period, an octagonal church containing a vaulted roof with an opening (oculus) in the middle was built on the site. At its center point—some 2.5 meters west of the center of the Byzantine church—a stone chapel, or aedicule, supported by columns with elegantly carved capitals encircled the footprints. Although a number of scholars have previously assumed that the arches of the Crusader aedicule were originally left open, it is now known that the aedicule was walled.[71] The upper part of the chapel may have been open to the sky, as was the church above it, but the sources are unclear. The drum and dome, as well as the interior of the

---

71. Pringle indicates, "It is clear, now that the render which formerly covered it has been removed, the ashlar filling the arcade is bounded with the corner pilasters and was an original part of the structure." Pringle, *Churches*, 81.

chapel containing the mihrab, date to the seventeenth century. While the Crusaders enshrined the footprints of Jesus and at least had an opening in the roof of the church, the visual continuity between footprints and sky that marked the pre-Crusader experience was significantly restricted.[72]

Following Saladin's conquest of Jerusalem in 1187, the church was converted into a mosque, with modifications to the aedicule made by the Ottomans in the seventeenth century. Although it is not mentioned in the Quran, Muslims believe that Jesus ascended into heaven as a living human being and is the only prophet that will return to earth. There is a prayer niche (mihrab) inside the chapel, and the site remains in Muslim hands.

The Chapel of the Ascension is a Status Quo site, with five Christian communities having the right of liturgical usage for their respective feasts of the Ascension that includes an overnight vigil (one Western: Franciscan; four Eastern: Greek, Armenian, Coptic, and Syrian). Makeshift chapels, oriented to the east, are set up around their respective altars, along with awnings and tents: the Franciscans erect their altar inside the aedicule. The Chapel of the Ascension is a unique example of a shared religious site.[73]

PILGRIMAGE TEXTS: THE ASCENSION

Epiphanius, *Holy City* 33 (before 692): And farther on to the east there are 2,340 steps going up to the Place of Teaching in which Christ taught the apostles saying, "I am about to be taken up. And as for you, go and teach the things I have taught you." Not far to the north of the Place of Teaching is a church, in the middle of which is the stone where Christ stood when he was taken up, and it is called the Holy Stone.

Adomnán (Arculf), *On the Holy Places* 1.23 (c. 680): Nowhere on the whole Mount of Olives does one find a higher place than the one from which it is said that the Lord ascended into the heavens. A great round church stands there, which has round it three porticoes with vaulted roofs. But there is no vault or roof over the central part: it is out of doors and open to the sky. At the east of it has been built an altar with a small roof over it.

---

72. See Pringle, *Churches*, 72–88.

73. On the ascension site, see Pringle, *Churches*, 72–88; Aist, *Christian Topography*, 202–15; Murphy-O'Connor, *Holy Land*, 141–43; Schick, *Christian Communities*, 354–55. Our understanding of the history of the complex, in particular, the Byzantine church, was significantly changed and clarified by the excavations of Father Virgilio Corbo in 1959.

The Stations

The reason why there is no roof over the inner part of this building is so as not to hinder those who pray there from seeing the way, from the last place where the Lord's feet were standing, when he was taken up to heaven in a cloud, to the heavenly height.... Holy Arculf was a constant pilgrim at this place, and reports that [the footprints are] situated, as we have explained, inside a large circular bronze railing, which is about the height of a man's neck, according to the measurements. In the center there is a sizable opening through which one looks down and sees the Lord's footprints plainly and clearly impressed in the dust. On the west of the circular railing is a kind of floor, which is always open, and enables people to go in and approach the place of the holy dust, reach their hands down through a hole in the railing, and take grains of the holy dust....

[The footprints] cannot be covered either with a roof, nor with any other sort of covering, high up or low down, in order that it shall always remain visible to pilgrims, and that the prints of the Lord's feet can clearly be pointed out there. A great lamp hangs above the circular railing from a pulley, and lights the footprints of the Lord, burning day and night.

On the west of the round building described above are eight upper windows paned with glass. Inside the windows... are eight lamps.... These lamps shine out from their windows on the summit of the Mount of Olives with such brilliance, that they light up not only the part of the Mount to the west, near this round stone church, but also the steps leading all the way up from the Valley of Jehoshaphat to the city of Jerusalem, which are lighted, however dark the night....

Every year, on the anniversary of the Lord's Ascension, when it is noon, and the holy ceremonies of the Mass in this church are over, a violent storm of wind bursts in, so violent that no one can either stand or sit in the church or anywhere near it. People remain lying on their faces until this terrifying storm has passed over. The Lord's footprints are still clearly to be seen in the opening in the middle of the circular railing we have described, and this remains open to the sky.... [On] the night of the feast of the Lord's Ascension, they add innumerable other lamps there, besides the eight which burn in this round church every night. Their solemn and marvellous brilliance pours out through the window panes not only to illuminate the Mount of Olives, but also, as it seems, to set it on fire and to light up the whole area of the city below and its surroundings.

Hugeburc (Willibald), *Life of Willibald* **21 (724–26):** From [the church where Jesus prayed, Willibald] went to a church on the mountain itself, where the Lord ascended into heaven: in the centre of it is a square brass thing which is beautifully engraved. It is in the centre of the church where the Lord ascended into heaven. And in the middle of the brass thing is a square lantern with a small candle inside: the lantern encloses the candle on all sides. It is enclosed in this way so it will continue to burn, rain or fine. That church has no roof, and is open to the sky. Inside it, against the north and south walls stand two columns, to remind people of the two men who said, "Ye men of Galilee, why gaze ye into the sky?" Any one who can creep between the wall and the column is freed from his sins.

Bernard, *Journey to the Holy Places* **15 (870):** On the top of this mountain, and a mile away from the Valley of Jehoshaphat, is the place where the Lord ascended to the Father. The church there is round and has no roof, and in the middle of it, at the place of the Lord's ascension, is an open-air altar at which they celebrate the rites of the Mass.

SCRIPTURE READINGS: THE ASCENSION

Luke 24:50–53: Then [Jesus] led them out as far as Bethany, and, lifting up his hands, he blessed them. While he was blessing them, he withdrew from them and was carried up into heaven. And they worshiped him, and returned to Jerusalem with great joy; and they were continually in the temple blessing God.

Acts 1:3–12: After his suffering [Jesus] presented himself alive to them by many convincing proofs, appearing to them during forty days and speaking about the kingdom of God. While staying with them, he ordered them not to leave Jerusalem, but to wait there for the promise of the Father. "This," he said, "is what you have heard from me; for John baptized with water, but you will be baptized with the Holy Spirit not many days from now." So when they had come together, they asked him, "Lord, is this the time when you will restore the kingdom to Israel?" He replied, "It is not for you to know the times or periods that the Father has set by his own authority. But you will receive power when the Holy Spirit has come upon you; and you will be my witnesses in Jerusalem, in all Judea and Samaria, and to the ends of the earth." When he had said this, as they were watching, he was lifted up, and a cloud took him out of their sight. While he was going and they were gazing up toward heaven, suddenly two men in white robes stood by them. They said, "Men of Galilee, why do you stand looking up toward heaven? This Jesus, who has been taken up from you into heaven, will come in the same way as you saw him go into heaven." Then they returned to Jerusalem from the mount called Olivet, which is near Jerusalem, a sabbath day's journey away.

Concluding the Circuit

The Jerusalem Circuit ends with the place of Jesus' ascension, which turns our eyes—and then our feet—back to the city of Jerusalem. Before we hurry off, the completion of the Circuit invites us to linger for a moment, to celebrate the journey, to create a final memory. Pilgrims find time and space to reflect on events, exploring language to describe experience, giving meaning to our moments with God.

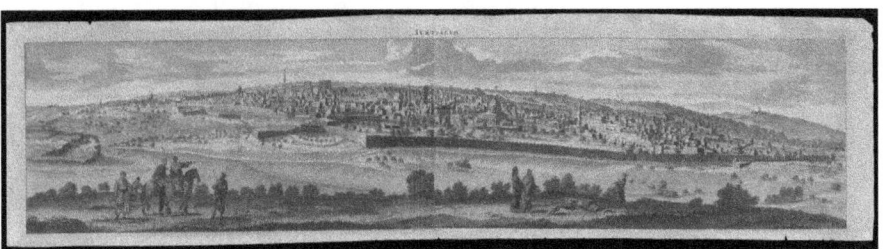

Fig. 24. *Ierusalem*, 1698. Cornelis de Bruyn (Dutch, 1652–1726/7). Copperplate. The Eran Laor Map Cartographic Collection. The National Library of Israel. Public domain.

WHILE STILL ON THE MOUNT OF OLIVES

Savor the completion of the Circuit in simple ways.

- Let your eyes take the lead: find a place to absorb the breathtaking view of Jerusalem.
- Recall the words of Sophronius: "[Let me] regard the beauty of the Holy City lying over to the west. How sweet it is to see thy fair beauty, City of God, from the Mount of Olives!"

- Say a prayer over the city. Pray for the peace of Jerusalem.
- Relish the blisters, sweat, and sore feet.
- Take more photos; do a piece to camera; make a sketch of the city; write a letter to yourself.
- Have a drink or a coffee; perhaps some baklava will do.
- Mark your departure from the Mount of Olives.

RETURNING HOME

There are at least four possible ways to walk back to Jerusalem. The same steps up are the simplest way down. The second easiest route is an additional two hundred meters past the top of the steps: continue south on the road along the ridge of the Mount of Olives until you come to a landing of steps on the right that leads to a tarmac descent. The road, which passes the Church of Dominus Flevit, descends to Gethsemane. A third option, al-Mansourieh Street, which is approximately fifty meters to the right from the Chapel of the Ascension, *should be avoided*: the narrow road is busy with traffic and lacks sidewalks. A fourth alternative is the A-Tur Road further to the north: going right from the Chapel of the Ascension, walk along the main road, Rabi'a al-Adawiya Street, for seven hundred meters (ten minutes) until you come to a traffic light, which is A-Tur Junction. Take the road to the left (A-Tur Road) down the Mount of Olives to the Kidron Valley and up a steep hill to the northeast corner of the Old City.

FURTHER REFLECTIONS

Mark Twain wrote with regard to Jerusalem, "We do not think in the holy places; we think in bed, afterwards, when the glare and the noise and the confusion are gone."[74] Greater reflection occurs away from the sites after the Circuit is over.

- What are your general thoughts and reflections on the Circuit? What connections and emotions, conversations and stories, interactions and incidents do you remember?

---

74. Twain, *Innocents Abroad*, ch. 55.

- What insights, takeaways, and new perspectives did the Circuit reveal? What did you learn?
- In what ways did the Circuit surprise, confuse, or confirm your thoughts, knowledge, and experience of Jerusalem, past and present? What questions did it raise?
- How did you experience the interaction between people, place, and story at specific sites and throughout the walk?
- Reflect on Jesus' ascension as the concluding narrative of the Jerusalem Circuit. What was it like to have the place of the ascension as the final destination of the walk? How does the ascension story inform the Christian life? What perspective does it give to Christian pilgrimage?
- Reflect on Christian Jerusalem, past and present. How might the Christian experience of Jerusalem contribute to ecumenical and interfaith relations in positive ways?
- What's next?
- Share your stories and reflections with others.

"Then they returned to Jerusalem from the mount called Olivet..." (Acts 1:12).

4.

Bibliography

FURTHER READING

On the Byzantine circuit of Jerusalem, see Wilkinson, "Christian Pilgrims," and Aist, *The Christian Topography*, which expands the discussion to the Early Islamic period. For English translations of the pilgrimage texts: in the late 1800s, the Palestine Pilgrims' Text Society (PPTS) of London published several volumes, all available online. More recent translations of the pre-Crusader texts, including the principal sources of the Jerusalem Circuit, are contained in Wilkinson, *Jerusalem Pilgrims*. For translations of Egeria, see McGowan and Bradshaw, *The Pilgrimage of Egeria*, and Wilkinson, *Egeria's Travels*. For Crusader texts, see Wilkinson, *Jerusalem Pilgrimage*, works by Pringle listed below, and the relevant volumes of the PPTS.

The starting point for the archaeology of the Christian sites of Jerusalem is Murphy-O'Connor, *The Holy Land*; for more detailed discussions of the pre-Crusader material, see Aist, *The Christian Topography*; Pringle, *Churches*; and Schick, *The Christian Communities*. On plans of pre-Crusader Jerusalem, see *The Illustrated Atlas of Jerusalem*, also published as *The Carta Jerusalem Atlas*, by Bahat and Rubenstein. For "footsteps of Jesus" approaches to Jerusalem, see Pixner, *With Jesus in Jerusalem*, and Walker, *In the Steps of Jesus*. Websites that focus on the holy sites include www.biblewalks.com and seetheholyland.net.

On the contemporary art of the Jerusalem churches, see Panzetta and Monicolini, *Italian Artists in the Holy Land*, and the websites of the

BIBLIOGRAPHY

Dormition Abbey, the Church of St. Anne, and the Basilica of Gethsemane listed in the book. For a contemporary approach to Holy Land pilgrimage including discussions on understanding the sites and the history of the Christian Holy Land, see Aist, *Jerusalem Bound*.

A number of these works, both ancient sources and older secondary literature, can be accessed for free on the Internet Archive (https://archive.org/). Also see the Internet Medieval Sourcebook administered by Fordham University (https://sourcebooks.fordham.edu).

ANCIENT SOURCES

Adomnán. *On the Holy Places*. In *Adamnan's De Locis Sanctis*, translated by Denis Meehan. Dublin: Dublin Institute for Advanced Studies, 1958. Also in *Jerusalem Pilgrims Before the Crusades*, translated by John Wilkinson, 167–206. Warminster: Aris & Phillips, 2002.

Ambrose. *On the Death of Theodosius*. In *Funeral Orations by Saint Gregory Nazianzen and Saint Ambrose*, translated by Roy J. Deferrari, 303–32. New York: Fathers of the Church, 1953. https://archive.org/details/fathersofthechur012812mbp/page/n329/mode/2up?view=theater.

The Armenian Guide. In *Jerusalem Pilgrims Before the Crusades*, translated by John Wilkinson, 164–66. Warminster: Aris & Phillips, 2002.

The Armenian Lectionary. In *Egeria's Travels*, translated by John Wilkinson, 175–94. Warminster: Aris & Phillips, 1999.

Bede. *On the Holy Places*. In *Jerusalem Pilgrims Before the Crusades*, translated by John Wilkinson, 216–30. Warminster: Aris & Phillips, 2002.

Belard of Ascoli. *Guide*. In *Jerusalem Pilgrimage, 1099–1185*, translated by John Wilkinson, 228–32. London: Hakluyt Society, 1988.

Bernard the Monk. *A Journey to the Holy Places*. In *Jerusalem Pilgrims Before the Crusades*, translated by John Wilkinson, 260–69. Warminster: Aris & Phillips, 2002.

Bordeaux Pilgrim. *Travels*. In *Egeria's Travels*, translated by John Wilkinson, 26–34. Warminster: Aris & Phillips, 1999.

Breviarius (A and B). In *Jerusalem Pilgrims Before the Crusades*, translated by John Wilkinson, 117–21. Warminster: Aris & Phillips, 2002.

Commemoratorium. In *Jerusalem Pilgrims Before the Crusades*, translated by John Wilkinson, 252–57. Warminster: Aris & Phillips, 2002.

Cyril of Jerusalem. *Catechesis*. In *The Works of Saint Cyril of Jerusalem*. 2 vols. Translated by Leo P. McCauley and Anthony A. Stephenson. Washington, DC: The Catholic University of America Press, 1969–70.

Daniel the Abbot. *The Pilgrimage of Daniel the Monk*. In *Jerusalem Pilgrimage, 1099–1185*, translated by John Wilkinson, 120–71. London: Hakluyt Society, 1988.

Egeria. *Travels*. In *Egeria's Travels*, translated by John Wilkinson. Warminster: Aris & Phillips, 1999. Also see Anne McGowan and Paul F. Bradshaw. *The Pilgrimage of Egeria: A New Translation of the Itinerarium Egeriae with Introduction and Commentary*. Collegeville, MN: Liturgical, 2018.

Bibliography

Epiphanius the Monk. *The Holy City and the Holy Place*. In *Jerusalem Pilgrims Before the Crusades*, translated by John Wilkinson, 207–15. Warminster: Aris & Phillips, 2002.

Eucherius. *Letter to Faustus*. In *Jerusalem Pilgrims Before the Crusades*, translated by John Wilkinson, 94–98. Warminster: Aris & Phillips, 2002.

Eusebius. *Church History*. In *Eusebius: The Church History*, translated by Paul L. Maier. Grand Rapids: Kregel, 1999.

———. *In Praise of Constantine*. In *In Praise of Constantine: A Historical Study and New Translation of Eusebius' Tricennial Orations*. Translated by H. A. Drake. Berkeley: University of California Press, 1976.

———. *Life of Constantine*. Translated by Averil Cameron and Stuart G. Hall. Oxford: Clarendon, 1999. Excerpts in *Egeria's Travels*, translated by John Wilkinson, 16–22. Warminster: Aris & Phillips, 1999.

———. *Onomasticon*. In *Palestine in the Fourth Century A.D.: The Onomasticon by Eusebius of Caesarea*, translated by G. S. P. Freeman-Grenville. Edited and introduced by Joan E. Taylor. Jerusalem: Carta, 2003.

Hugeburc. *The Life of Willibald*. In *Jerusalem Pilgrims Before the Crusades*, translated by John Wilkinson, 233–51. Warminster: Aris & Phillips, 2002. In *The Anglo-Saxon Missionaries in Germany*, translated by C. H. Talbot, 151–77. London: 1954. (Reprinted in *Soldiers of Christ: Saints and Saints' Lives from Late Antiquity and the Early Middle Ages*, by T. F. X. Noble and T. Head, 141–64. University Park: Penn State Press, 1994).

Jerome. *The Book of Places*. In *Palestine in the Fourth Century A.D.: The Onomasticon by Eusebius of Caesarea*, translated by G. S. P. Freeman-Grenville. Edited and introduced by Joan E. Taylor. Jerusalem: Carta, 2003.

———. *Hebrew Questions on Genesis*. In *Jerome: Hebrew Questions on Genesis*. Edited and translated by C. T. R. Hayward. Oxford: Oxford University Press, 1995.

———. *Letters*. In *St. Jerome: Letters and Selected Works*. Translated by W. H. Freemantle. Grand Rapids: Eerdmans, 1995.

John of Würzburg. *Description of the Holy Land*. In *Jerusalem Pilgrimage, 1099–1185*, translated by John Wilkinson, 244–73. London: Hakluyt Society, 1988.

John Rufus. *The Life of Peter the Iberian*. Excerpts in *Jerusalem Pilgrims Before the Crusades*, translated by John Wilkinson, 99–102. Warminster: Aris & Phillips, 2002.

Josephus. *The Jewish War*. In *Josephus*, vol. 3. Translated by H. St. J. Thackeray. Loeb Classical Library 210. Cambridge: Harvard University Press, 1927–28.

Nikulás of þverá. *Extract from Nikulás of þverá*. In *Jerusalem Pilgrimage, 1099–1185*, translated by John Wilkinson, 215–18. London: Hakluyt Society, 1988.

Origen. *Commentary on St. John*. In *Origen: Commentary on the Gospel According to John, Books 1–10*. Translated by Ronald E. Heine. Washington, DC: Catholic University of America Press, 1989.

———. *Commentary on St. Matthew*. In *The Commentary of Origen on the Gospel of St. Matthew*. 2 vols. Translated by Ronald E. Heine. Oxford: Oxford University Press, 2018.

Paulinus of Nola. *Letters*. In *Letters of St. Paulinus of Nola*. Vol. 2. Translated by P. G. Walsh. Westminster, MD: Newman, 1967.

The Piacenza Pilgrim. *Travels*. In *Jerusalem Pilgrims Before the Crusades*, translated by John Wilkinson, 129–51. Warminster: Aris & Phillips, 2002. Also see the translation by Andrew S. Jacobs: https://andrewjacobs.org/translations/piacenzapilgrim.html.

Procopius of Caesarea. *On Buildings*. In *Jerusalem Pilgrims Before the Crusades*, partially translated by John Wilkinson, 124–38. Warminster: Aris & Phillips, 2002.

The Protevangelium of James. In *The Protevangelium of James*. Introduced, edited, and translated by J. K. Elliott, with a commentary by Patricia M. Rumsey. Brepols Library of Christian Sources 3. Turnhout: Brepols, 2022.

Saewulf. *The Pilgrimage of Saewulf*. In *Jerusalem Pilgrimage, 1099–1185*, translated by John Wilkinson, 94–116. London: Hakluyt Society, 1988.

Second Guide. In *Jerusalem Pilgrimage, 1099–1185*, translated by John Wilkinson, 238–43. London: Hakluyt Society, 1988.

Sophronius. *Anacreontica*. In *Jerusalem Pilgrims Before the Crusades*, translated by John Wilkinson, 157–63. Warminster: Aris & Phillips, 2002.

———. *Life of Mary the Egyptian*. Internet Medieval Sourcebook. https://sourcebooks.fordham.edu/basis/maryegypt.asp.

Theodosius. *The Topography of the Holy Land*. In *Jerusalem Pilgrims Before the Crusades*, translated by John Wilkinson, 103–16. Warminster: Aris & Phillips, 2002.

MODERN SOURCES

Aist, Rodney. *The Christian Topography of Early Islamic Jerusalem: The Evidence of Willibald of Eichstätt (700–787 CE)*. Studia Traditionis Theologiae 2. Turnhout: Brepols, 2009.

———. *From Topography to Text: The Image of Jerusalem in the Writings of Eucherius, Adomnán and Bede*. Studia Traditionis Theologiae 30. Turnhout: Brepols, 2018.

———. *Jerusalem Bound: How to Be a Pilgrim in the Holy Land*. Eugene, OR: Cascade, 2020.

———. "The Monument of the Miraculous Healing in Post-Byzantine Jerusalem: A Reassessment of the North Gate Column of the Madaba Map." *Bulletin of the Anglo-Israel Archaeological Society* 26 (2008) 37–56.

———. *Pilgrim Spirituality: Defining Pilgrimage Again for the First Time*. Eugene, OR: Cascade, 2022.

Bahat, Dan, and Chaim T. Rubenstein. *The Carta Jerusalem Atlas*. 3rd ed. Jerusalem: Carta, 2011.

Biddle, Martin. *The Tomb of Christ*. Gloucestershire: Sutton, 1999.

Borgehammar, Stephan. *How the Holy Cross Was Found*. Stockholm: Almqvist & Wiksell, 1991.

Cohen, Raymond. *Saving the Holy Sepulchre: How Rival Christians Came Together to Rescue Their Holiest Shrine*. Oxford: Oxford University Press, 2008.

Cohen-Hattab, Kobi. "Struggles at Holy Sites and Their Outcomes: The Evolution of the Western Wall Plaza in Jerusalem." *Journal of Heritage Tourism* 5:2 (2010) 125–39.

Drijvers, Jan Willem. *Helena Augusta: The Mother of Constantine and the Legend of Her Finding the True Cross*. Leiden: Brill, 1992.

Freeman-Grenville. G. S. P., trans. *Palestine in the Fourth Century A.D.: The Onomasticon by Eusebius of Caesarea*. Edited and introduced by Joan E. Taylor. Jerusalem: Carta, 2003.

Gibson, Shimon, and Joan E. Taylor. *Beneath the Church of the Holy Sepulchre, Jerusalem: The Archaeology and Early History of Traditional Golgotha*. London: Palestine Exploration Fund, 1994.

Bibliography

Hillner, Julia. *Helena Augusta: Mother of the Empire*. Oxford: Oxford University Press, 2022.

Inge, John. *A Christian Theology of Place*. Aldershot: Ashgate, 2003.

Lemire, Vincent. *In the Shadow of the Wall: The Life and Death of Jerusalem's Maghrebi Quarter, 1187–1967*. Redwood City, CA: Stanford University Press, 2023.

Limor, Ora. "The Origins of a Tradition: King David's Tomb on Mount Zion." *Traditio* 44 (1988) 453–62.

Magness, Jodi. *Jerusalem Through the Ages: From Its Beginnings to the Crusades*. Oxford: Oxford University Press, 2024.

Murphy-O'Connor, Jerome. "The Cenacle and the Community: The Background of Acts 2:44–5." In *Keys to Jerusalem: Collected Essays*, 123–33. Oxford: Oxford University Press, 2012.

———. *The Holy Land: An Archaeological Guide from the Earliest Times to 1700*. 5th ed. Oxford: Oxford University Press, 2008.

———. *Keys to Jerusalem: Collected Essays*. Oxford: Oxford University Press, 2012.

———. "Tracing the Via Dolorosa." In *Keys to Jerusalem: Collected Essays*, 107–22. Oxford: Oxford University Press, 2012.

———. "What Really Happened at Gethsemane?" In *Keys to Jerusalem: Collected Essays*, 77–106. Oxford: Oxford University Press, 2012.

Panzetta, Alfonso, and Gianluca Monicolini, eds. *Italian Artists in the Holy Land: Routes and Itineraries of Contemporary Italian Art in the Holy Sites*. Jerusalem: Alpha Studio, 2018.

Pinkerfeld, Jacob. "'David's Tomb': Notes on the History of the Building; Preliminary Report." In *Bulletin of the Louis Rabinowitz Fund for the Exploration of Ancient Synagogues* 3, edited by Michael Avi-Yonah, 41–43. Jerusalem: Hebrew University, 1960.

Pixner, Bargil. *With Jesus in Jerusalem: His First and Last Days in Judea*. Corazin, Israel: Corazin, 1992.

Pringle, Denys. *The Churches of the Crusader Kingdom of Jerusalem: A Corpus*. Vol. 3: *The City of Jerusalem*. Cambridge: Cambridge University Press, 2007.

———. *Pilgrimage to Jerusalem and the Holy Land, 1187–1291*. Crusade Texts in Translation 23. London: Routledge, 2018.

———. *Three Pilgrimages to the Holy Land: Saewulf, John of Würzburg, and Theoderic*. Corpus Christianorum in Translation 41. Turnhout: Brepols, 2022.

Romney, Kristin. "Jesus' Burial Tomb Uncovered: Here's What Scientists Saw Inside." *National Geographic*, Oct. 28, 2016. https://www.nationalgeographic.com/premium/article/jesus-christ-tomb-burial-church-holy-sepulchre.

Schick, Robert. *The Christian Communities of Palestine from Byzantine to Islamic Rule: A Historical and Archaeological Study*. Princeton, NJ: Darwin, 1995.

Shoemaker, Stephen J. *Ancient Traditions of the Virgin Mary's Dormition and Assumption*. Oxford: Oxford University Press, 2002.

Stern, E., ed. *The New Encyclopedia of Archaeological Excavations in the Holy Land*. Vol. 2. New York: Simon & Schuster, 1993.

Storme, Albert. *Gethsemane*. 2nd ed. Translated by Gerard Bushell. Jerusalem: Franciscan Printing, 1972.

Twain, Mark. *Innocents Abroad, or the New Pilgrims' Progress*. Hartford, CT: American, 1869.

Bibliography

Walker, Peter. *In the Steps of Jesus: An Illustrated Guide to the Places of the Holy Land.* Oxford: Lion Hudson, 2007.

Wilken, Robert L. *The Land Called Holy.* New Haven, CT: Yale University Press, 1992.

Wilkinson, John. "Christian Pilgrims in Jerusalem During the Byzantine Period." *Palestine Exploration Quarterly* 108 (1976) 75–101.

———. *Egeria's Travels.* 3rd ed. Warminster: Aris & Phillips, 2002.

———. *Jerusalem as Jesus Knew It: Archeology as Evidence.* London: Thames and Hudson, 1978.

———. *Jerusalem Pilgrimage, 1099–1185.* With J. Hill and W. F. Ryan. London: Hakluyt Society, 1988.

———. *Jerusalem Pilgrims Before the Crusades.* 2nd ed. Warminster: Aris & Phillips, 2002.

www.ingramcontent.com/pod-product-compliance
Lightning Source LLC
Chambersburg PA
CBHW020851160426
43192CB00007B/877